Stop Smoking Easily
and Transform Your Life
for Good

Stop Smoking Easily and Transform Your Life for Good

Elliott Wald

www.easystop.com

Stop Smoking Easily and Transform Your Life for Good

Wald, Elliott
Stop Smoking Easily and Transform Your Life for Good
Bibliography

ISBN 10: 1-934266-05-1
ISBN 13: 978-1-934266-05-2

Library of Congress Cataloging-in-Publication Data
Wald, Elliott
Stop Smoking Easily and Transform Your Life for Good
Includes bibliography.
    1.Smoking 2. Stop Smoking 3. Smoking Cessation
RC567.W_   2008   613.8

Published by:
Network 3000 Publishing Co.
3432 Denmark, PMB 108
Eagan, MN 55123
USA
(612) 616-0732
Phone Toll Free: 1-888-707-1896
Fax: 651-365-0524

This book is dedicated to the four people
I love most in the world,
my amazing wife Tracy, you complete me,
my three beautiful children
Aaron, Amber and Piers

Contents

Acknowledgements   ix

About the author   x

Foreword   xiii

Introduction   xv

How to use this book   xvii

Part 1: Make Up Your Mind to Stop Smoking

1   The crunch decision   3

2   Shocking! The smoker just digs in   9

3   What do you really want?   18

4   Get real about your beliefs   20

5   The solution, not the problem   24

6   Oh, the illusions   25

7   The most successful way to fail   27

8   The choice is yours   29

9   What next?   33

Part 2: Stop Smoking

10   Your mind is amazing   39

11   Escape from the smoking trap   42

12   Changing beliefs? that's easy   44

13   What have you missed?   50

14   Supercharge your motivation   52

15   Is it imagined or is it real?   59

16	Focus before action	67
17	Conscious and unconscious	74
18	The seven illusions of smoking	80
	Illusion one: Willpower	83
	Illusion two: Smoking relaxes you	85
	Illusion three: You enjoy smoking	88
	Illusion four: Smoking gives you confidence	89
	Illusion five: Something to do with your hands	90
	Illusion six: It's a habit	90
	Illusion seven: The weed fights the fat	95
19	Putting it together	96

Part 3: Staying Stopped

20	Never again	103
21	Inoculate yourself	105
22	Staying a winner	108

Warning! You have stopped smoking.
Read the rest of the book only if you want to achieve
more powerful, positive and permanent changes
in other areas of your life

Part 4: Change Your Life for Good

23	Now you have a springboard	113
24	Achieving the goals	123
25	Down to you	128
26	No fear	140
27	Resources all around	149
28	Giving is receiving	167
29	What does success mean to you?	174

Bibliography	179

Acknowledgements

Thank you to all the people who have helped to make this book a reality, to all the EasyStop Consultants and staff around the world for their energy and passion. My thanks go to Ian Selby, Julian Selby, Ken Huggins and Paul Russell for believing in my message and recognising the value and importance of the EasyStop method, and to George Coghill for bringing life to the pictures I had in my mind and creating the outstanding illustrations contained within this book.

I want to thank all the teachers of human potential who have shared their knowledge with me and from whom I have had the great privilege to learn, including Dr Richard Bandler, Dr Rubin Battino, Michael Breen, Michael Carroll, Dr Deepak Chopra, Stephen Covey, Dr Robert Dilts, Dr Stephen Gillingham, Dr John Grinder, John La Valle, Igor Ledchowski, Paul McKenna, Michael Neil and Tony Robbins.

To my friends Adam Eason and Richard Wells for their time and understanding.

About the author

How do people start smoking? We all have our own stories to tell and here is mine. My love affair with the weed began when I was an overweight 13-year-old schoolboy. My first surreptitious drags were at the bottom of the school football field, an area of land that could have been made for secret under-age smokers. The field had a gradual slope, which levelled out at just the right height so that you couldn't be seen.

We cunning pupils called this spot 'the bank', and, of course, it was out of bounds. This was a place where we were not allowed to tread, but I and the other cool kids would gather there before and after school for our smokes. This was the forbidden territory in which to be seen by your peers as one of the daring 'in crowd'.

I was not too sure of the reasons why I joined in this illicit practice. Perhaps the fat boy in me wanted to be accepted as cool and that ambition led me down the path to the bank and provided the overture to years of smoking. Or maybe I chose this brand of sin just because I wasn't allowed down the bank. Maybe there was a rebellious part of my personality that didn't like being told not to do something. This quirk was to surface years later as a fascination with human excellence, achievement and success. Maybe that rebellion triggered what was to become a 20-year love-hate relationship with tobacco.

Although I don't actually remember why I started the un-healthy habit, I do know that, years later, when all my school friends were gone, when school was a distant memory, when the building was levelled and the land covered by a housing estate, I was four stone overweight and puffing my way through 40 cigarettes every day.

One day that fascination with human excellence, achievement and success resurfaced with a vengeance. I went into overdrive, devouring hundreds of books on personal development and listening to audio programmes on human potential. I quickly learnt and understood that our Creator gave us an amazing powerful tool in the human mind and that we can do absolutely anything that any other human being has already succeeded in doing. After all, we all have similar neurology and DNA. As I delved deeper in my thirst for knowledge with my sights set on harnessing and using the power of the mind, it became clear to me that all human beings can change the embedded patterns and habits they have learnt, developed and practised over a lifetime. And I discovered that this can be done easily and permanently.

With continued passion I applied what I learnt and observed what worked and what didn't. I combined various techniques and found ways to make them work even better. I honed this process down to the very core to create an incredible method for controlling weight. This was something of a revolution as it involved changing the principles of how we think. Gradually all this mind activity paid off. I lost four stone and became a competitive body-builder. I had hit my target.

Then I switched the focus to my 40-a-day smoking habit. I had stopped counting the times I had tried to ditch those cigarettes. Once I stopped for eight hours and that wasn't even while I was sleeping! Another time I congratulated myself because I actually abstained for a week. However, soon enough I always gave myself another excuse to start again and so the struggle went on. I started to evaluate my smoking habit closely, discovering what was happening to me and why I did not find it easy to stop. I read hundreds of technical papers on tobacco and the effects of smoking as well as studying endless research papers and statistics on stopping. I wrote down what I was experiencing and started to engineer piece by piece a method to overcome every obstacle as it arose. I continued to read more self-development and psychology books by the ton, listened to thousands of hours of audio programmes, and travelled the world learning from the most eminent teachers on human potential. Then in 1996 came the summing-up. I combined all that I had discovered about smoking with the tools and techniques I had created to break the smoking cycle and produced a method to stop myself smoking, and indeed I stopped. And, surprise, surprise, I couldn't start smoking again because this time I had no desire to smoke, no desire for that old smouldering weed. It was easy. I had created a method that changed for ever the way I thought about smoking and, believe it or not, I enjoyed the stopping experience and the accomplishment itself.

It showed too. Friends noticed I was no longer smoking and was happy about it. They asked how I had kicked the cigarettes. So I showed them the method and they stopped too. The whole thing became contagious. Before long I was teaching others how to deliver the method. And they achieved the same amazing results. More and more people sought me out, asking me to teach them the process so that they could help others to stop. Even better news was to come. The EasyStop method was born, an easy and permanent way to stop smoking had been created and the EasyStop network of smoking cessation centres began to mushroom.

The consultants I trained soon gathered that I had once been four stone overweight and that I had shed the flab and kept it off. They asked how I did this. They asked me to teach them to help others to achieve the same great results, and the pattern we had established when people asked about beating smoking was repeated. They started helping people to lose weight with outstanding results.

And now as I commit all this to paper, EasyStop Consultants can be found successfully operating across the UK, the Philippines and in Australia. This network of professional consultants, helping smokers and weight clients to achieve their personal goals is the incredible reward that I enjoy every day. I know that thousands of people are breaking free from smoking or losing their excess pounds, thanks to a method that works. Like me, they have proved its effectiveness and are enjoying its benefits.

Foreword

I once encountered a man who had been hospitalised by his smoking habit. He had smoked so much that it had caused his heart to fail and he wound up in hospital with a smoking-related heart disorder. While in hospital, knowing that he could possibly be killing himself, he sneaked into the hospital gardens and lit up a cigarette, such was his addiction.

Can you think of anything more motivating to stop smoking than the true, bare face of death? Forget the messages on packets, the scary images in advertisements or the frightening statistics. This guy was shown the end and was committed to hospital and kept alive – yet that was still not enough to get him to stop smoking.

As a therapist, how could I possibly deal with a habit, an addiction that seemingly possessed people in this way?

Over the years, with my work at The Hypnotherapy Association, through my books and speaking at events worldwide, I have met hundreds and hundreds of therapists. They all deal with a wide variety of clients and see people for some of the most complex illnesses and behavioural issues known to man.

Almost none of them claim to relish dealing with an individual to help them to stop smoking. A smoker represents a very serious challenge to the vast majority of therapists. I have even met therapists who welcomed the smoking ban here in England with a sense of foreboding! Many therapists seem to lack a sense of conviction in the methods they use and doubt their own abilities with this wicked habit, a habit that seems to dig its claws into even the most determined individual and refuses to let go, regardless of how serious that individual's motivation seems to be.

Then along came Elliott Wald.

I first met Elliott a number of years ago at a training course. I was so taken by his contagious drive, enthusiasm and belief in the methodology that he had created for helping people to stop smoking, I enrolled in his own training. It was inspiring.

It is impressive enough that Elliott created the EasyStop method, the brand and the company that is the face of modern stop-smoking cessation clinics. However, that was not what did it for me. What got me buzzing with excitement was the eclectic gathering and combination of differing aspects of modern psychology and personal development that are used in such a brilliant and easily applicable way.

I began using that very technique with great success with my own private clients and it revolutionised my practice.

Now all of those things, and more, have been put into this book and made easily accessible for anyone and everyone to apply. I think it means a new dawn has arrived. Old approaches to stopping really are becoming just that – old. This book represents a fresh, modern, vibrant approach that all can apply to themselves to make tremendous change in their lives.

Every smoker who wants to stop smoking should read this book. Every health professional attempting to help a smoker to quit should recommend this book.

I love this book. When you use the strategies and techniques given in this book, you'll be an ex-smoker – what's more, you'll be a far fuller expression of yourself than you may have imagined and you certainly know how to do so much more with that amazing bio-genetic computer residing inside your head. I recommend you read it and re-read it and tell friends what it was that finally enabled you to take control once and for all.

Adam Eason
Author of *Secrets of Self-Hypnosis*

Introduction

Stopping smoking is easy. Yes, believe me, it is easy and it can be easy for you. You've heard so many pessimists say the opposite and maybe you have believed them. Perhaps you have gritted your teeth and tried to stop. After miserable failure you may be thinking: 'It was far from easy the last time I tried.'

Yet I can assure you that stopping is easy if you approach it in the right way. If you simultaneously deal with the physical addiction and the psychological dependence, if you change the way you think and feel about smoking, then it's easy.

Think of a chain with a padlock attached. If you use the right key the padlock opens, freeing you for ever. If you use the wrong key you can force as much as you like but you won't get the chains off. The more you try the more it frustrates you. You stay locked in and trapped until eventually you stop trying and you believe it's just too hard to stop.

Many so-called experts will try to tell you it is difficult to stop smoking. Many smokers may declare with authority that it is difficult, and unfortunately many medical professionals will also give you that line, based on their experience of other methods of stopping. Ways and means differ, but 82 per cent of smokers who have used the EasyStop method confirm it was easy.

And it doesn't matter whether you have been smoking for less than a year or for more than 70 years, or any length of time in between. You can quit, easily and permanently.

It doesn't matter if you are young or old, male or female. You can break out of the smoking trap and remain free from cigarettes for ever.

It doesn't matter if you smoke fewer than ten cigarettes a day or more than 50. Yes, incredible as it seems, some people do manage to squeeze 60 or more smokes into every 24-hour period. The method recommended in this book will work for them too.

It doesn't matter if this is your very first attempt to stop smoking or your 100th. This time you can succeed and you will succeed.

Forget, too, about the usual aids, artificial or otherwise. You will find it easy to stop without willpower, without patches, without chewing gum, without pills, without lasers, without acupuncture and above all, without withdrawal pangs, weight gain or adverse side effects. You will be able to draw a line under your old life as a smoker. You will gain the benefit of better health and longer life, and you will have more money to spend on other real pleasures.

Everyday 300 people in Britain wave goodbye to their cigarettes for ever. They are no different from you. They have stopped already and soon you will be like them. By 2007 the EasyStop method had helped many thousands around the world for 12 years to stop smoking easily and permanently.

This book will act as your personal coach and will help you every step of the way to achieve your goal and become one of the thousands of happy ex-smokers. It contains all of the tips, tools and techniques you will need to stop smoking easily and to stay stopped for good. This book contains everything you need for your own personal success.

Enjoy the book and enjoy a lifetime of freedom.

How to use this book

You may ask what makes the EasyStop method any different. For starters, this book is based on 12 years' practical experience accumulated from helping thousands of smokers to stop smoking easily. Just accept that the method works and it will work for you. At worst, you have nothing to lose. It is like setting out on a journey with a route map. To reach your destination, just follow the route map.

As you proceed on this journey through the book, it is important that you follow all the instructions and exercises. This is vital if you are going to finish your journey in the correct place and be a happy ex-smoker. The only smoker who cannot succeed with this method is the one who doesn't follow all the instructions. If the book asks you to stop reading and do something, then stop reading and do it. This is vital for your success.

One little discipline is to have a highlighter or pen handy so that you can personalise this book. You will make it truly your own manual when you underline the parts that provide enlightenment or create a change, parts that you may want to refer to from time to time as you change your life. When there are pages to complete, fill them in as requested. This is another part of the method that will help to clear tobacco out of your life.

Your book is divided into three sections – how to make up your mind to stop smoking, how to stop smoking, and how to enjoy your new smoke-free life. It is by no means an accident that the method is called EasyStop. That is exactly what it is. Easy. You will soon light your last cigarette and stop smoking for good. The next section of the book is about making your mind up.

MAKE YOUR MIND UP TO STOP SMOKING

CHAPTER 1

The crunch decision

So now it's decision time. It's time to take that first step. Are you pondering, considering, weighing up, thinking about or simply mulling over whether you want to stop smoking? Maybe you're trying to decide whether this is something you should do, want to do, or even can do. You may be saying to yourself: 'I'll give stopping smoking a go.' If these are your attitudes you won't have much of a chance of kicking out tobacco because you haven't fully made up your mind to do it yet. So read on.

On the other hand, you could go for it with all guns blazing. This could be your big day. A day when you decide to stop smoking and leave yourself no alternative to that resolve, you pile-drive in the foundation on which to succeed. If this is the big day you will have built something strong and positive that you feel compelled to follow.

There must be none of the wishy-washy stuff. This may all sound dramatic but you must make that decision with all you've got and commit yourself 100 per cent to that decision. You must also get it into your head that this is more than a decision. It's a feeling and a knowing. Think back to those other occasions when you have determined to do something, maybe learning to drive or ride a bicycle, or even turning around a business. The total commitment you gave it guaranteed your success. If that sounds dramatic to you, then so be it. Remember, if quitting smoking is on the agenda, health and life itself may be at stake. It's bigger than driving and riding and making a profit.

You can't listen to mixed messages. You can't stop by allowing some parts of you to be focused on stopping smoking while other parts are unsure and in a state of limbo. If you have that solid commitment and unwavering sense of purpose, every part of you will be heading in the same direction, with the same intent. At the same time you must allow your mind to access your inner resources. They may be lying dormant within you but you have to recruit them and pull them into the campaign.

That is how the ground must be prepared. Every part of you has to be working with you and for you, so your mind is made up to stop smoking for ever.

Now for a soundbite. In more than ten years of helping people to stop smoking, we have learnt that every smoker is different, and yet every smoker is the same. No, that's not double Dutch. Let me explain. Smokers are all different in that they may have started smoking for different reasons, they are different because they may smoke different quantities or at different times. All smokers are different because they may have a preference for different brands; they are different because they may have different associations, triggers or what you may call habits. And yet all smokers are the same because something makes them carry on smoking.

With or without their differences, smokers fall into three main categories:

1. Smokers who have never considered stopping before.
2. Smokers who have tried to stop many times and not succeeded yet.
3. Smokers who have convinced themselves that stopping is impossible for them.

Just for a moment think of cigarettes as being successful fishermen. For fishermen to catch the fish they must use the right bait and the correct rod. They must calculate the strength of the line, and have knowledge of the fishes' habits, their environment and what the experts call the 'swim'. Thus the canny fishermen know exactly how to catch the fish. That's just what those cunning cigarettes did to you. Make sense? They caught you, but unlike the fishermen who let their fish go, they kept you hooked and trapped. Smokers are the victims caught in the trap. If you are a smoker you are a victim too. It's just like that invisible chain with a padlock attached.

If you are going to escape from the trap, you must first fully understand how the trap works and how it keeps you trapped. You have been caught in the smoking trap by the lure of illusory pleasures, clever advertising and external influences. We call this the hooked, caught and netted process. It's dangerous and it's highly successful, as millions of smokers will tell you – if they're honest.

Let's assume for the moment that you are reading this book because you have at the very least some interest in stopping smoking. Maybe you are nodding your head and thinking to yourself, 'I will do it one day perhaps not today, but one day in the future, maybe some time soon.' Just for the moment, it does not matter. That will do for now. Just keep on reading.

The intention of this section is not to stop you smoking, although some of you may do just that after reading it. The intention right now is to help you to make up your mind to stop and more importantly, to make up your mind to stay stopped. The harm goes on relentlessly if you have a stop-start pattern.

It is a fact of life that if you really want to keep on smoking, it is your personal choice. However, it *is* a choice, and before you choose to do something, especially something as important as this, doesn't it make sense for you to consider all your options first? Of course you should.

There is so much to consider too. Your decision may be one of the most important choices you will ever make, so think seriously when you are weighing up your options. The decision is a particularly important one for the loved ones who are relying on you and may be left behind grieving should you be one of the unlucky ones who pay the ultimate price. It shouldn't take too much head-scratching, but the choice has got to be yours. Nobody can make the choice for you.

This personal story from me may help. When I was a 40-a-day man, I had so many well-meaning people telling me why I should stop smoking. They're infuriating, aren't they? We've all had that tut-tut, finger-wagging counselling. This only made me more defiant to keep doing what I wanted to. That's human nature and it was certainly mine. I often thought I would actually keep on smoking just to show these people I was right all along and not give them the satisfaction of knowing that they were right all

along. I know it was bloody-minded of me, and how daft can you get! If you are thinking straight you take notice of the message, not the messenger. I managed to ignore the messages.

Therefore, please do not do this. I used to hate listening to all the wise advice and my natural response was to smile politely and ignore anything that they said. I still hate that scenario, so please don't let a bunch of well-meaning people be a reason for you to continue to smoke when you do not have to. However, this is not about right or wrong or about winning points. In some cases stopping smoking is a matter of life and death. Perhaps that puts a different complexion on your choice.

Hear this too. Once I had stopped smoking, all this anger and frustration and righteousness just drained away with the tobacco. These counterproductive emotions were pushed aside by the feeling of relief at letting go and experiencing the end of the constant battling to be right. That was some relief, a huge reward for making the right decision.

The decision is the first big landmark. Are you ready for it? When you make your decision to stop smoking, you will have taken the first and most important step.

Take this moment to think about what you believe. What you believe about smoking and what you believe about stopping smoking are so important.

As you continue reading I am going to ask you to question some of your own beliefs about smoking. I'll ask you to consider some of your beliefs about what smoking actually provides for you and why you continue puffing away, even though you may be in control in all the other areas of your life. It may not surprise you to know what a contrast exists in your life. You may be as tough as old boots when you control the staff in your office or discipline your children. Yet you feel robbed of power by a packet of cigarettes.

Don't worry. What I am not going to do is to tell you that smoking is bad for your health, that it causes cancer, sexual dysfunction, blindness or even premature death. Again, don't worry. That other pious advice is not coming your way! I am not going to tell you how much hard-earned cash you spend in a year or have spent over the years if you smoke 20 a day. You can work that one out for yourself and you know perfectly well that this money stops going down the drain the moment your smoking stops. I am not going to tell you all this because you already know it. I have never met smokers who thought smoking was good for them or provided excellent value for money.

This information about the dangers has been rammed down your throat along with the smoke so many times, day in and day out, that you probably don't even hear it any more. I would not be at all surprised if you have become deaf to all this information. In fact, I heard that in a survey of smokers, blindness was cited as the most feared health risk. When I was a smoker I would have heard this, but not heard it, and it wouldn't have dawned on me that smoking could cause a smoker to lose his sight. That's how deaf and blinkered the smoker becomes. It's a state of unreality.

You are an intelligent person, you can read the warnings on the packs, or at least you used to be able to before they became invisible to you. So if any of this information and preaching was going to help you to stop you would have done so already, wouldn't you?

CHAPTER 2

Shocking! The smoker just digs in

As a smoker you have to endure the scare tactics, the smoking bans and those frightening commercials. You may even have been hardened in your resolve to continue to smoke. Indeed, some of the advertising campaigns I have seen on television are so ridiculous that I have to ask myself whether they are telling people not to smoke or encouraging smokers to smoke more. Don't the advertisers realise that when smokers are told they must stop, it only makes them dig their heels? So you can forget those anti-smoking commercials. As you read through this book you are going to make up your mind to stop smoking for ever and set yourself free.

Then there is that pointless imposition of prohibition. For some years we have been hearing about smoking bans and they are an absolute nonsense! Bans only cause smokers to have a drag outside, and more often than not a smoker who would have smoked only one cigarette inside will now smoke two outside. Just watch the office workers standing on the pavement, squeezing in that extra cigarette before the break ends.

Scare tactics have similarly ineffective results. Commercials intended to make you terrified of dying from smoking or developing a serious illness only increase anxiety, making cigarettes and smoking even more precious and valuable in the smoker's mind. Sorry to pour cold water over good intentions but it seems the government is advertising on behalf of the tobacco companies. The cigarette manufacturers must be rubbing their hands every time the health gurus announce a new campaign.

Clearly, scaremongering and force of will only make smokers more defiant, more resistant, more panicky and more likely to hold on to their habit more tightly. It's sad for the government health advertisers, but they may even be making people smoke a few more than they did before. Trying to force a smoker to stop can be like cornering a cat. Don't be surprised if you get scratched.

I know it is not the smokers' fault. It is not entirely your fault that you started smoking in the first place as the smoking trap is subtle and sinister. Nor is it your fault that you have continued to smoke for so long. The smoking trap creates an array of illusions so powerful and deceivingly real that it is easy to be swept along year after year. The illusions of smoking are formidable enemies.

But take heart. An illusion or a trick is just that. Once you know how it is done and how the trick works it loses its hold over you and is stripped of all its power.

Also take heart from knowing that smokers really are the victims here, so you are a victim too. Admittedly, you did start smoking yourself, for whatever reason you had at the time, and, yes, you have continued to smoke. You must now take full responsibility for that. However, the cigarette manufacturers and marketers must not be allowed to get away scot-free. Some responsibility must surely lie with the people who have been pumping out the product to trap us for the past 30 years. Through their clever marketing campaigns and insidious product placement in movies we have all been conditioned to believe that cigarettes are valuable and that smoking is enjoyable and provides us with immense pleasure.

The deception goes on. What impression would you get from the heavy cut glass ashtrays? Don't they suggest the habit has some class and glamour? Just look at the packaging. Some of the packs are actually gold or silver in colour, and what do we associate with gold and silver?

The advertising and placements indicate that it is trendy to be seen with some brands. These are the luxury brands with matching aftershave, brands for the smoker who can afford the best in cigarettes. These suggestions are part of the 'styling' package.

Perhaps you can even remember cigarette brands that sponsored the big sporting events televised for all to see, or celebrated sportsmen smoking their brands on peak-time telly. Tobacco companies have sponsored cricket, darts and snooker tournaments, and, famously, Formula 1 racing. We have all seen cars emblazoned with cigarette advertisements zooming past on prime-time television. Wouldn't you feel slick doing the same, and smoking the 'right' cigarettes? The list of sponsorships meant to persuade and trick us is endless.

And what about the ultimate smoker, the man who smokes until the very end, the condemned man in a Hollywood movie? At the moment of death, rather than waving farewell to his wife or blowing a kiss to his children or taking his last deep breath of fresh air before he is shot or falls off the edge of the world, what does the wretched convict do? You've got it. He reaches into his pocket and pulls out a pack of cigarettes. He fumbles about for a lighter and lights one. Then he puffs it as if it is the most enjoyable and pleasurable thing he can do to finish his life. It's the only way to go!

Isn't that absurd? We are convinced of the desirability of the absurd, yet that's the power of marketing. What did you understand from these clever images? Did they tell you how valuable and pleasurable smoking must be if a condemned man wants to spend his final moments with a cigarette? The mind absorbs this as reality and may even believe this to be true. Yet in the cold light of day, without the subtle persuaders, you must believe this is quite absurd.

Think back to when you were a child. Do you remember waiting inside a sweet shop all those years ago? As a child you know this is the place where you go to be presented with your treats and rewards for having been good. While you are standing there, adults amble into this mini-pleasure palace, buying what must be goodies, because you're in the place where all manner of goodies are kept. What are the adults coming in for? Just watch – they are buying their cigarettes from the big display way up there behind the counter. The illusory association has started. You are already thinking that these must be the rewards for grown-ups, the goodies they enjoy, just as you love your humbugs and fudge. You may never have thought about it before, but doesn't selling sweets and cigarettes in the same shop convey a message to the impressionable?

The next step in this subtle process is watching the adults smoke. As children we see the expression of sheer satisfaction and pleasure as the adults suck lungful after lungful of smoke deep down into their lungs. We start to think: 'Oh boy, when I get older I am not going to miss out on those. They look great.' Such is the illusion, and the absurdity.

I know that as a child I wanted to buy those little white candies with the red tips so that my pals and I could really play 'grown-up'. When we could not get the candies we used a pencil, but we were nevertheless acting like grown-ups. The ploy of selling sweets and cigarettes side by side, if it was a ploy, was working.

For a moment, imagine that you have never smoked. You walk into a store and the man selling the cigarettes is under a magic spell compelling him to tell you the truth. It's pure fantasy and you don't have to believe it, but just step into this world for a moment.

You look up inquisitively at the small square boxes on the shelf and you ask: 'What are those?' The shopkeeper replies: 'Those are cigarettes, my young friend.' You ask: 'What are they for?' The shopkeeper says: 'They are for smoking.'

Now, here's the interesting bit, even if it is the stuff of dreams. 'And what do they do for you?' you ask. 'Well, my young friend,' he says, 'they smell unpleasant, and the smell lingers on your body. Smoking stains your teeth. The chemicals hidden inside the paper damage your health and rob you of your breathing so that as you get older your lungs grind to a halt. They cause cancer and numerous other health problems. They stain the paintwork if you smoke them in your house, and they ruin your sense of taste and smell. At least, that way you may not notice the smell of them as much. It's rather like setting fire to money as you burn up a cigarette and it turns to ash. Eventually cigarettes sow seeds in your mind that make you think you can't stop.'

Would you buy a packet?

As a teenager you get a similar, but diluted, message. You are warned constantly: 'Don't you start smoking, will you? It is a dirty, dangerous habit that will damage your health and you will become addicted and end up smoking all your life.'

However, as a teenager you know this can't be true, can it? You find it hard to believe because you have seen with your own eyes the extreme pleasure that cigarettes provide. Smokers must be enjoying it, you believe. Why else would they continue to do it, 20 times a day, and continue to pay for it? There simply must be some benefits in it, or else why would they do it? Isn't that right? Otherwise it would be madness, wouldn't it? Yet more illusion and absurdity.

Yet something does not make sense. Luckily, there is this little niggle, like a chink in the armour.

Smokers know deep down that they don't really want to smoke and if they could stop they would. They tell themselves they enjoy it and yet inside they wish they had never started smoking in the first place.

Let us approach it from a different angle. A friend of yours is thinking about starting smoking. What would you say to him?

I remember a conversation I had with my daughter years ago when I was still smoking. The exchange illustrates the point.

'It's very odd, Daddy,' said my daughter. 'You say that you smoke because you enjoy it, but you tell Mummy that you have cut down to five a day and you are going to stop soon. If you like doing it why do you want to cut down and stop? At school today we had a lesson about how bad drugs are and we were told we should say no to drugs.'

'That's good,' I said. 'You should never take drugs. They are dangerous.'

'But nicotine is a drug, Daddy, and you smoke and that's bad, isn't it?'

'Yes, sweetie, I know. But don't worry – Daddy's going to stop soon.'

Ouch! In this embarrassing corner I would swiftly and deftly change the subject as I knew I was not telling the truth. Like all smokers, I didn't want anyone to see how trapped I was.

The old saying that 'out of the mouths of babes and sucklings comes truth' ran through my mind. My daughter had hit home because we do know that nicotine is a drug and we do know it is addictive. Hence the difficulty you face as a smoker if you want to advise a friend.

This is how a drug addiction works. The user takes his dose of the drug and within a very short time, literally moments, he receives an artificial high. For a time he feels comfortable. Then the drug begins to leave the body and the user starts to feel a little agitated, a little anxious. At this point the drug user seeks his next fix.

13

This is the cycle of smoking. The smoker inhales his cigarette and within a very short time, literally moments, he receives an artificial high. For a time he feels comfortable. Then the nicotine begins to leave the body and the smoker starts to feel a little agitated, a little anxious. At this point the smoker seeks his next fix.

It's pretty obvious, isn't it? The drug cycle and the smoking cycle are the same and what's more, when the smoker relieves the feeling of agitation by having a cigarette so that he can feel relaxed again, he is topping up his drug levels. This process is repeated again and again. And guess who gets all the credit. The cigarette, of course, because it made the jumpy feeling go away.

For you, the smoker, the pattern is set. Every time you light a cigarette you guarantee that without doubt or question those feelings that you now call cravings will be back again soon. Thus you expose one of the illusions. Smoking is actually the cause of the uncomfortable feelings, not the cure.

Next, we'll deal with what you believe because what you believe is very important.

Lisa learns to swim

I have a friend. We'll call her Lisa. She believed that she could not swim. You might say that surely that didn't matter too much.

To put it another way, she believed she could never learn to swim, and she was right, because this was what she really believed. And perhaps you may feel the same way about stopping smoking right now, maybe you believe that you can't do it.

However, there was no physical reason why Lisa could not swim. And we all know that if she possessed enough desire, and sought out an expert instructor who was experienced in helping people to learn how to swim, she could do it. So could we all if we felt that way.

Then it would only be a matter of time before she would be able to swim and then she would be able to swim for ever, of course, Lisa did not think like that. Thanks to some little traumas she had her own belief about her ability to swim and she had created her own reality. These were mental blocks, so Lisa's belief that she could not swim mattered a lot, and subsequently it was to matter even more.

She had tried to swim previously, but she got water in her face, she struggled and splashed about, and because swimming was new to her, she found it embarrassing. She felt people were laughing at her and that was really hurtful. She said it was painful for her, and then she stopped trying. In her mind she knew she couldn't do it, even though she really wanted to swim. Her hurt did not end there.

She had allowed external pressures to influence her and she had hit a mental brick wall. So she never went swimming. Whenever she was asked to go swimming she would always make excuses, saying she did not like the water or suchlike, even though she knew this was not true. She fell into her own propaganda trap. She said it so many times that she started to believe it herself, and consequently she accepted it. What she believed became her reality and it would stay this way until she changed or overcame what she believed and created new beliefs.

Lisa soon had children, and as they grew up they started swimming lessons at school. Like all normal children they wanted their mum to take them swimming. It was inevitable that things would begin to get difficult. Lisa's children could not understand why all their friends' mums could swim and their mum could not. Would you say again that it does not matter? Try telling the children that. Youngsters are sensitive about this kind of thing and their mother felt uneasy too.

Seeing the other children playing in the pool with their mums and dads had a dramatic impact on Lisa. She loved her children dearly and wanted to do the best she could for them and set them an example. She did not want to miss out on having a good time with them. All this is natural enough, and this is what hurt most.

An important point here is that people will often do far more for the sake of their children and loved ones than they will do for themselves. The maternal instinct is a mighty force.

The story progressed this way. Every time Lisa heard the splashing of water it brought memories streaming back for her, memories of the experiences she had had in her previous attempts. She relived those associated feelings of fear, failure and embarrassment. This emotional learning from her experiences had conditioned her to respond in certain ways, ways that drove her to make excuses to stay out of the water and away from the pool. A friend would say: 'Come on, let's go swimming. You'll love it.' Lisa would murmur: 'I really don't like it. It's just not my thing.' Yet deep in her heart she wished she had learnt, so that she could live the life she wanted, and have more fun with her children and be free, no longer hiding scared and fooling herself. The ability to swim would have lifted this burden for ever.

Decision day did eventually come. That day Lisa resolved to be free of the fear and she knew the only option for her was to take lessons and learn to swim. The love for her children had won. It's no exaggeration to say the decision was life-changing.

She was scared, of course. It was to be expected because she didn't know that she could do it. She had tried before and failed and she was comfortable not swimming. For her that was normality. Yet it was far from normal for a young mum. She had all the emotions of embarrassment and fear, but she stood firm and made that decision, the decision that something must be done. Merely thinking about it would never would set her free and give her what she really wanted.

Having made the decision to learn, Lisa got on with it and was soon swimming and having fun with her kids. She had that confident feeling that a weighty burden had been lifted and the hurt just went away. The swimming instructor told Lisa that when she was young she had learnt how 'not to swim' rather than learning 'how to swim'. As a consequence, 'not swimming' had become a way of life for her. Now they were behind her, all these hidden fears of failure and of the unknown future characterised by such statements as 'I don't like swimming', or 'It's not my thing', or 'Yeah, maybe one day'.

The moral is that a genuine decision can achieve the desired result.

From beekeeper to world explorer

Edmund Hillary, now Sir Edmund, was a beekeeper living in New Zealand with a fascination with climbing. In 1952 Hillary failed in his attempt to climb the 29,000ft Mount Everest. A couple of weeks later he was asked to speak at a public engagement. Hillary walked on to the stage, made a determined fist, pointed at a photograph of the mountain and declared: 'Mount Everest, you beat me the first time, but I'll beat you the next time because you've grown all you're going to grow, but I'm still growing.'

The gritty Hillary had committed himself in front of an audience. A year later he conquered Everest, becoming, with Sherpa Tenzing, the first to reach the summit of the world's highest mountain. Afterwards he said: 'Never at any stage until we actually got up the rock step was I confident that we were going to be successful. My feeling was that we would give it everything we had, but we had no surety that we were going to reach the top. In fact, I believe that if someone starts out on a challenging activity, completely confident that they're going to succeed, why bother starting? It's not much of a challenge. I think it's much better to start out on something that you're not at all sure that you can do. If you overcome and you manage to defeat the obstacles, the satisfaction is so much greater.'

I remember being told: 'If you are going to think about something, then you may as well think about what you want, and think big!'

Most of our beliefs are learnt from our past experiences or even from our future when we start to imagine how something might be. By speculating about the future we start creating a self-fulfilling prophecy and we shape our beliefs accordingly. For smokers there is a particular lesson. They have learnt and may also believe that it is difficult to stop smoking, yet don't they know there are many smokers who have already stopped? They may take a defensive stance and may say: 'Well, it was different for them.' Perhaps they will tell you: 'Oh, they didn't smoke for as many years as me.' Or they declare, as if it makes any difference: 'They only smoked ten a day.' In taking such attitudes smokers continue to shape their beliefs.

CHAPTER 3
What do you want really want?

You already know that if you liked or enjoyed doing something you would want to do more of it. It stands to reason that you certainly wouldn't want to do less of it or cut down on the activity or tell everyone that you will stop doing it soon. You wouldn't want to avoid it. You know that would be crazy, don't you? Why don't you do more of it then? The fact is that even if you think you like smoking, you don't. Of course, it can seem as if you like smoking, and that's the whole point.

Smokers always delude themselves. The American writer Elbert Hubbard said, with a great deal of wisdom: 'It has always been a mystery to me why people spend so much time deliberately fooling themselves by creating alibis to cover their weakness. If used differently, this same time would be sufficient to cure the weakness. Then no alibis would be needed.'

You will make some instant progress if you answered two questions.

Question 1: Are you pleased that you started smoking in the first place?

Question 2: If you knew of a way to stop smoking that could make it easy and permanent, and you would not have to spend the rest of your life as an old misery missing your cigarettes, would you do it?

We all fully appreciate that wanting something is sometimes not enough. I suspect that even though you may want to stop smoking you just can't imagine life without cigarettes. Try to imagine that now, a life without cigarettes. This shows you the vice-like grip tobacco can have on you. I agree there are a few obstacles to overcome if you are going to chuck the weed for good. Together they may seem daunting, but broken down and overcome step by step the process can be easy, and that's where EasyStop comes in.

CHAPTER 4
Get real about your beliefs

How would you manage to live your life without cigarettes? Is it hard to imagine an existence minus those little comforters? Would you still be able to smile? Sure you would. There truly is a lot more to life, isn't there? So what's holding you back? How do you think non-smokers cope with life, without cigarettes?

It can be all too easy to crumble at the first sign of an obstacle. Every day obstacles, big and small, lie in front of us in everything that we do. In particular, we curse the obstacles that stand in the way of those things that we seem to desire the most or seem the most elusive. They certainly make life challenging but nobody ever said our time on earth would be a walk in the park. Without some challenges there would be no satisfaction or feelings of accomplishment when we achieved our goals and experienced success. So welcome some challenges.

Back to beliefs again. Imagine that we wanted to achieve or obtain something in life, something important, and yet we have created beliefs in our minds that we cannot have it or achieve it because of the obstacles that we already see are in the way, whatever these obstacles may be. It is likely therefore, that we do not achieve it or get it. That's like a mantra, but it's a negative one. You may not appreciate it when you say to yourself that this or that is possible or impossible, but the biggest obstacle in your mind, no matter what it is that you desire, is usually fear-based. Stopping smoking is no different.

There is the fear of loss, the fear of failure, the fear of how to cope. Those fears nag at us, make us shake and possibly even appear to affect us physically. However concrete those fears may seem, the first thing to remember is that a fear is not real, because it is essentially a thought. The object of a fear hasn't happened. A fear is something that we think might happen some time in the future, and as we think about it we have already dreamt up the worst-case scenario. These fears that loom ominously in our imagination feel just like reality because our mind cannot tell the difference between reality and imagination. This is the incredible state you may be in, all thanks to fear.

Try this experiment in order to understand the power of fear. Imagine you are walking home alone late at night, it's pitch black and nobody is around but all of a sudden you feel as though you are in a Hitchcock film, as the victim. In the distance you think you hear footsteps. Your heartbeat accelerates, your breathing rate increases, and you listen a little harder. Hitchcock's still doing his stuff because you hear the footsteps getting louder and closer. Your heart is beating like a drum now and you turn around quickly. There is nobody behind you. Your stalker was in your head. What a good thing there was no audience! Your imagination had created a fear that was so real that you experienced a measurable change in your physical state. Your pulse and blood pressure readings would have been quite frightening.

The same process occurs when you think about stopping smoking. Similar fears, created by your imagination, quickly rise to the surface and create an anxiety that leads to what you believe is a desire to smoke. A fear that started in a small way but was fuelled by other thoughts made smoking appear to be all the more important to you. As I said earlier, what you believe is of the utmost importance.

At this moment you can continue to smoke as I take you through the steps towards making up your mind to free yourself for ever, and you must believe you can do it. It's a case of belief again.

Now don't regress into the obstacle mentality. The method you are holding in your hands right now is easy and will help you to create a permanent and positive change. It is nothing like the jumping-off-the-cliff method or the running-into-the-brick-wall method that you may have tried before, because you can carry on smoking while you read this book and follow the programme. It couldn't be easier, even if you believe that you may be a touch weak, although I am sure there were also times when you believed that you were not. That's why it's called the EasyStop method. What I do need is for you to possess a genuine desire to stop smoking and stay stopped. Now that's quite simple.

Fearful? Is your imagination playing that trick on you again? Believe me, there is nothing for you to fear, and as you continue to read this book that will become clearer. I bet you can think of some really scary pictures in your mind where you feel this fear and yet I also know that you can quickly imagine times when you felt strong or happy in certain situations and you felt confident. What you believe in your mind is powerful and easy to change. And as you change the way you think, you will change the way you feel about smoking. As your behaviours change, you will see smoking in a new light.

Were you honest with yourself when I asked you the first question? Are you actually pleased that you started smoking in the first place? That is a fantastic starting point; you really wish you did not smoke. Imagine how great it would feel if you could go back in time and make a different choice and be smoke-free.

It is important that you continue giving honest answers to yourself when we consider some of the reasons why you have not tried to stop smoking before or why you have not succeeded in stopping. This is a time for you to discover some new information for yourself about what you really believe.

Many smokers promise: 'I am going to do it tomorrow.' As a smoker I know that 'tomorrow' is a tactic that I employed to get well-meaning people off my case. I gave the transparent 'tomorrow' promise many times. In fact, I said it so often that I actually believed it myself. It's a cliché, but we all know that the tomorrow we talk about so confidently never comes.

The confidence was false and I was only deluding myself. That delusion was in good company, or should I say bad company? It joined a few others in my life. I deluded myself about how many cigarettes I was smoking. I deluded myself that I wasn't harming anyone else. That argument no longer holds when you see how much lung disease is blamed on second-hand smoke. I even deluded myself by not accepting that smoking was harming me. We can all point to the exception to the rule. There's old Charlie who smoked 30 a day and lived healthily to the grand old age of 85. However, that was old Charlie, or some other ancient smoker, not me. I used the example to kid myself that I might be one of the lucky ones. 'Problems from smoking? It won't happen to me,' I would say.

CHAPTER 5
The solution, not the problem

One of the most important steps to making up your mind is to realise stopping smoking is the solution. Stopping is what you want to move towards. Smoking is the problem you should move away from. A philosophical maxim is that we do everything out of either our need to avoid pain or our desire to gain pleasure. It's not actual pain that makes our decision, but our fear that something will lead to pain. Smokers believe that stopping smoking is painful and difficult, focusing on the short-term benefits, rather than the long-term rewards. That is why we say that stopping smoking is the solution and smoking itself is the problem. After all, if smoking was not the problem, you would not want to stop doing it, would you?

Here is another example of aiming for the goal. Try to remember when you were a child and you were looking forward to the annual family vacation. The holiday was booked, the date was set, you had your passport, you had seen the hotel with an inviting pool in the brochure, and you could hardly wait for the day to dawn.

You were so excited that you were bursting at the seams. You started to count down the days, and with every day you became more excited still, and there was never any way that you would say: 'Hey, guess what. I have decided not to go on holiday after all. I have decided to stay here at home and clean my room.' No way, because the holiday was what you wanted.

CHAPTER 6
Oh, the illusions

Do you remember right at the beginning of the book that I told you about the hooked, caught and captured process of smoking? Now you can probably see how smoking grabbed hold of you. Not only have you been caught, but you have also been locked in tight by its false charms.

Let me explain for a moment some of the ways in which cigarettes have kept you trapped in this prison. We'll pretend for a moment that smoking just creates a collection of powerful yet subtle illusions for smokers. The dictionary describes an illusion as a wrong or misinterpreted perception of a sensory experience, a false idea or belief – in other words, something that you believe to be true or real but isn't.

Although they are not reality, illusions can have an extremely powerful effect. You have probably watched a master magician sawing a woman in half. You see the feet and head completely separated, and you feel with part of you that it has actually happened. Or a huge elephant simply vanishes into thin air. These magicians just mesmerise the audience. Now, I have a friend who is a master magician and a member of the Magic Circle. This man is really amazing to watch. One day I asked him to teach me a couple of illusions as my daughter was having a birthday party and I wanted her friends to see some tricks. He started by demonstrating the trick on me. It looked so real, and because of the skill with which he performed it even felt real. Then he showed me how it was done. It was so simple and yet so powerful. However, as soon as I understood how the illusion worked, the trick just didn't have the same hold over me.

The truth is that when you find out the solution to a puzzle, or discover how an illusion or trick works, then that illusion or trick simply loses all its power and hold over you.

The relevance of all that is that smoking is the master of illusion. It has created a number of illusions for you. They are illusions that you may still believe are true, but they are illusions that we are not going to help you to dispel during this first section. Nevertheless, we are going to make you aware of them. As with every good trick, one of the keys is misdirection of the audience, a shift in their attention, if you like.

Smoking subtly offers us seven key illusions. Below are the seven illusions creating the misdirection that makes you think that tobacco actually does things for you that it doesn't. They are:

- That it takes willpower to stop smoking.
- That smoking helps you to relax, or it alleviates stress.
- That smokers like smoking or enjoy it.
- That it's a habit that smokers have had for so long that they can't stop.
- That smoking gives you confidence.
- That smokers need something to do with their hands.
- That you will gain weight when you stop smoking.

These are all just illusions, tricks of the mind that at the moment probably may seem real. When you discover how these illusions work you won't believe a word of it. I expect you've heard people mention these illusions a thousand times. Later in the book I will show you how to dispel these illusions for yourself, and once you do this you will automatically change the way you think about smoking. Then, because you fully understand how the illusions work, they will never have the same hold over you again.

This is only the first step on your stop-smoking journey. Perhaps you have already begun to move towards the point where you really do want to stop smoking or maybe you are just starting to think a little more about it than you did before.

CHAPTER 7

The most successful way to fail

It may seem odd but I want to look at failure techniques. If you are raising an eyebrow, that's understandable, but just bear with me.

This is the reason why I'm considering the negatives. If you think or expect you are going to fail you will probably seek out the quickest and most convenient way you can find to stop smoking. It is a common sly ruse of smokers whose only real desire is to shake off well-meaning people so that they can say they tried. After promptly failing, they can get on with their smoking with that 'I told you so' look on their face.

The funny thing is that these smokers do not fail at all. In an upside down kind of way they are very successful. They can chalk up several victories on the board. They succeed in showing everyone that they were going to try something and they did that. They succeed in failing quickly and they succeed in being able to smoke again. What is more, they actually find the quickest and most convenient way to carry on smoking by using the most effective way to fail. Is this reasoning beginning to make sense now?

In psychology there is a technique called the law of comparisons. In order to make a comparison and ultimately a decision you must have more than one option. Most people would call this plain common sense without any psychological overtones. Anyway, let's examine two options.

When you started smoking did you think you would be at it for as long as you have been? Did you really think you would continue for five, ten, 20 or more years? It probably never entered your mind, did it? So if you didn't think then about your future as a smoker, you probably haven't thought about your next five, ten or 20 years with the habit. You're not alone. Most people wouldn't give it a thought either.

Now let's take a smoker's journey into the future. What could smoking right up to the end do for you? Imagine your life five years from now if you continue to smoke. Try to think what condition your body will be in after 20 cigarettes a day for those five years. You will have smoked at least another 35,000 cigarettes. After that onslaught what would this have done to your health? Maybe you will feel you are breathing a little more heavily. Think about what you would see, and what you would hear. And how would you feel? Does this peep into the crystal ball trouble you at all?

We'll jump forward five more years so that we are looking at you ten years from now. You are even more breathless. You really notice the old lungs struggling as you climb the stairs or walk from your car or trot around the shops. We notice that your skin has tightened a little and is now drying up. As you look more closely into that crystal ball maybe you notice there are fewer smokers around now, so you are feeling more alone and even more trapped than you do now. Repeat the exercise to observe what is happening to you, to listen to your breathing and coughing, and to see how you are feeling.

Have a peek at your reflection in the mirror. You look so haggard, and you're wheezing a little, aren't you? As you look closer you see your teeth have started to yellow. It must be scary to see how all those years of smoking have taken their toll. Weigh up everything you have observed in your imaginary leap into the future and understand that this could be the result of your choice to continue to smoke.

CHAPTER 8
The choice is yours

Good news, I now want to consider your other option. You have made the choice to stop smoking. First came the decision, then the action, and now you've fished out that crystal ball again. You are gazing at yourself five years from now, and you are seeing yourself after five smoke-free years. I'm sure you like what you see now. Your breathing has improved, along with your general health. In fact, your whole life has become more active, and you are happier. You spend more time with the family and you smell fresher and sweeter. With justification you feel that great sense of achievement, you experience a wonderful freedom, and you are brimming over with pride, but without being boastful, of course. There's no room for the self-righteous ex-smoker. By courtesy of the crystal ball you are seeing and hearing a new you and you are feeling how you would feel. You imagine taking a nice deep breath of fresh air and you notice how great that is.

Let us do what we did when you looked at the decrepit you, still on the smokes. We move forward five more years. After ten years you are even more pleased with yourself. Your skin looks fresher and healthier and is almost glowing. Another treat is your reflection in the mirror. You see yourself smiling back at you. Yes, you did it, and you have enjoyed the holidays that you now take instead of burning your money. Your whole family has benefited because you stopped smoking and you feel proud, seeing what you would see, hearing what you would hear and feeling how it really feels to be rid of smoking.

Now we are starting to make progress on your stop smoking journey. We have started to dismantle some of the fundamental parts of the smoking trap that has imprisoned you for so long. Maybe you can already start to see smoking for what it really is and now that you are armed with this information you are closer to making the right choice, the right decision for you.

The more information the better of course, and there is more information that you will need if you are to make a good choice. Smoking has two roots that have been holding you in the smoking trap, and for you to break free from the trap both have to be tackled. If you deal with only one you might as well be chopping the head off a weed. Any good gardener will tell you that if you hack off the head and leave the roots intact the weed will grow back sooner or later, and maybe stronger.

One of these enemies is the physical root. This is the physical addiction to nicotine and the many other chemicals contained in cigarettes. The other, the psychological root, is even more important. It has many sides to it. It is composed of your belief structure, your automatic behaviour and your other behaviour patterns, and the associations and triggers that link your activities with your smoking. This last aspect is so familiar to smokers. A man may say: 'As soon as I get bad news I simply must have a cigarette.' This is the kind of link we must sever.

Time for a recap. What have we covered so far?

- That smoking is a trick and the benefits of smoking are illusions.
- That if you are honest with yourself you want to stop smoking.
- That smoking is the problem and stopping smoking is the solution.
- That thousands of people have stopped smoking.
- That to stop smoking permanently you must remove both roots.

Those points above are basic facts about smoking. The rest of this book will help you to take action to remove both roots so that you can stop smoking and stay stopped for good and feel great.

Life is always about making choices. Continuing to smoke and stopping smoking are both choices. It's your choice if you want to continue to smoke, and you know where this road leads, and it's your choice to make your mind up to stop smoking, to reach a decision and to take action now. The story below illustrates the importance of choice.

John in the air

John was in the window seat in the aeroplane and he was not happy. The source of his understandable discontent was something quite reasonable but that didn't stop it being infuriating. John had been forced by security measures to check in at Newark, New Jersey, three hours before flight time. In boring circumstances that just grind on you, you do things you would not normally dream of. John had watched an entire in-flight movie. That was a killer. He had read the airline house magazine from cover to cover. Equally, a waste of time. On the brighter side he had enjoyed the quiet professionalism of the cabin crew as they served meals and drinks to him. He was delighted that the Airbus 600 to Heathrow was almost an hour ahead of its scheduled time thanks to the westerly jet stream five miles above the Atlantic. But he was still not happy.

After landing at Heathrow he bounded through the immigration and customs procedures as fast as he could. He almost broke into a run as he increased his pace through the doors leading into the Terminal 3 arrivals hall. He had done all this before, so he knew that a sharp right turn, underneath the meeters and greeters barrier, would take him to the coffee shop.

Did he want a coffee? No, he ignored the small queue at the counter and made for his favourite corner table. He plonked himself down heavily with a sigh of relief. He reached urgently into his jacket pocket, pulled out a pack of cigarettes and a lighter. With indecent haste he tore off the wrapper, flipped the lid and thrust a cigarette in his mouth.

John allowed himself a little smile. He had made a choice, though choice was not really the word he should have selected. Ask any smoker to put himself in that position. In reality John had no choice even then, because he was a habitual smoker. He had just been through his own private hell. In a cold sweat he thought of how he had just endured almost eleven hours without a cigarette.

He was not alone. He knew that all the other passengers on his flight were similarly tired after their journey. Then he did a head count and realised that about a third of them, like him, were additionally stressed almost to breaking point. They, of course, were the other deprived smokers gagging for that first draw on a cigarette. And how John and those other passengers had suffered! Their habit turned every journey into an aching test of endurance rather than a relaxing experience to be enjoyed and treasured.

The absurdity then struck him. This, he thought, was just plain stupid. It was self-inflicted duress. Who wants to go through hours of agony? Like John, many of these people were regular travellers, whizzing off on business trips to Europe and the United States all the time. For them, and for John, the craving for a smoke had ruined the experience.

John stubbed out a longer than usual butt and headed for the counter to get his first espresso. He had read somewhere that, although most smokers had a cigarette with every cup of coffee, this actually lessened the charge of both the caffeine and the nicotine so that the desire for the next would come sooner rather than later.

By the time he had drained his cup there were three stubs in the ashtray. That was some going even for him. It was wake-up time. 'I'm not really daft,' he told himself. His next flight was a month away and he didn't want that horrible experience again. As he left the terminal building and breathed deeply in the crisp cool dawn air of early summer he knew he would remember this time and place for the moment of resolve they represented, for his positive and conscious decision to stop smoking once and for all.

John had taken the first crucial, and for many smokers, the most difficult step. He had made up his mind to stop smoking.

CHAPTER 9
What next?

Let's take a closer look at where you are right now. On a scale of 1 to 10, where 10 means you have made your mind up to stop smoking and 1 means you really want to keep on smoking, what number do you represent?

If you are a 7 or above, please carry on to the next section. If your number is 6 or below, read this section again until you have found the answers that you are looking for to make the right decision. On the following page you find a form. Fill it in now.

I HAVE MADE MY MIND UP TO STOP SMOKING
SOLEMN AND BINDING PROMISE

I [name] _____

do solemnly declare that I have made my mind up to stop smoking.

In return for the freedoms, improved health, and the social and financial benefits that are now within my reach permanently, with the best of my ability I undertake to:

Follow every instruction to the letter

Complete every simple exercise when I am asked to

Take action to become a permanent ex-smoker

Signed _____

Dated _____

Complete this page and read it every day as you journey towards your becoming a happy ex-smoker. It will remind you of your promise and commitment, and that will help you to stay on track.

You have made the right choice. You know it and I know it. So just take a moment to congratulate yourself on having made your mind up to stop smoking. Congratulate yourself on having moved forward to the second stage where you can stop smoking for ever.

Of course, I don't know, at which point in reading this book you will finally stub out your last cigarette and stop smoking for good. Perhaps you will follow the programme through completely before you stop, or you may simply find that you have already stopped before you complete the book. There is no set pattern, but you have already passed a landmark point and you are now heading in the right direction. So now let's move on.

STOP SMOKING

CHAPTER 10
Your mind is amazing

I am now going to give you a simple lesson in human biology. It will help you to understand what's happening to you. Your Creator blessed you with the most powerful computer in the world – your mind. Twenty-four hours a day, 365 days a year, you carry with you the most powerful learning machine the world has ever seen. Probably you have been told that from the cradle, or at least from your early school days.

Let me flesh out that information with some facts and figures that you probably don't have at your fingertips. The brain is capable of processing up to 30 billion items of information per second. Your nervous system contains about 28 billion neurons, and every neuron in itself is a computer that can process nearly a million items of information. As well as acting independently, every neuron can communicate with your other neurons through a chain of 100,000 miles of nerve fibres.

Not too stuffy and technical for you, is it? Contained within this powerful hardware is the software that runs the programmes and patterns determining your behaviour. Throughout your life your software has been downloading information at both a conscious level and an unconscious level. It continues to download every day and will do so for the rest of your life. You are receiving billions of pieces of information every second, your software prevents mass overload with an ingenious filtering process called your reticular activating system. This works like a heat-seeking missile whose role is to notice what is important to you. The software does this when any of the billions of pieces of information meets one or more of the following criteria:

- If your survival depends on it.
- It has strong emotional intensity.
- It offers pleasure and comfort rather than pain and discomfort.

As you can see, the power of your mind is truly amazing. Every thought, feeling and aspect of behaviour starts in the mind. Unfortunately, unlike your home computer, that wonderful machine inside your skull didn't come with a booklet of instructions telling you how best to operate it. Ever since *Homo sapiens* became a scientific creature he has been scratching his head to find the best way to organise it and put it to good use.

I'll continue with this basic human biology lesson by looking at how your mind works. Your mind is divided into left and right hemispheres. If you look down on the brain from the top, it resembles two halves of a walnut joined together. You've seen the pictures and diagrams, I'm sure.

This is what the division of the brain means to smokers. The left department is your logical, analytical side. As this section applies logic it is the side that knows you *should not* smoke. That section of the walnut on the right is your emotional side, the 'feeling' side. Because you're human you give in to the right side more often than not, because it 'feels right'. This is the side of your mind that makes you think you just want a cigarette or you just need one.

Confused? Sometimes this mental division can puzzle the owner of the brain, it's true. Your mind does send you mixed messages.

One side says: 'I know I should not smoke.'

The other side protests: 'But I just want one.'

The left warns: 'I know they are bad for me.'

The right responds appealingly: 'But I just fancy one.'

A constant battle is waging inside, making you weigh up the two sides. You've got your own personal tug of war. It's as if you have a little angel on one side and a little devil on the other. I'm sure you know what I mean, though you may not have thought about it in this way before.

CHAPTER 11

Escape from the smoking trap

We've talked about these two roots before. There may be some guidance in this tale from *Aesop's Fables*. A boy playing in the field was stung by a nettle. He ran home to his mother, telling her he had touched the nasty weed and it had stung him. 'It was just your touching it my boy,' said his mother, 'that caused it to sting you. The next time you meddle with a nettle grasp the weed tightly, pull it up by its root and it will do you no hurt.'

The two roots, as I've already said, are the physical, involving an addiction to nicotine and some of the other 4,000 chemical compounds in cigarette smoke, and the psychological, which shows up as a habit when you automatically light up after eating a meal, while speaking on the telephone or driving, or finishing off a drink. You may remember I said both had to be dealt with and both roots removed. Otherwise, it's like chopping off the head of a weed and allowing it to sprout again.

The guidelines in this book will show you how to do it right. They will show you how to attack and remove both these roots, making it easy for you to stop smoking for good.

Let's be rid of the psychological root first. A lot of research has been done in this area, but what it all boils down to is that when you take a certain action, and associate certain feelings or emotions with that action, it determines your behaviour. The equation is: action plus feelings equal behaviour. This meets one or more of the criteria of your reticular activating system.

The quiet but vigorous activity that I described going great guns in your brain is the backroom work that directs human behaviour. In practical terms it means that we seek pleasure and avoid pain, and when we do or we experience something that gives us pleasure, we seek it more. The opposite is true too, of course. When we do experience something that gives us pain it makes us feel uncomfortable and we avoid it.

I'll give you an example, but I'm sure you could find many more yourself from your own experience. You telephone a friend to whom you haven't spoken in a long time, and he says: 'Oh, so you do know how to use the phone.' Or he snaps out something else equally negative or sarcastic such as: 'You decide to call . . . at last.' You associate pain with the action of calling him. So you think to yourself: 'There's no point in phoning again if all he's going to do is moan.'

Alternatively, you telephone another friend to whom you haven't spoken for ages and he says: 'It's so nice to hear from you. Thanks for calling.' That's much better, isn't it? You associate pleasure with that action and you think: 'I enjoyed calling him and I'll call again soon.' You reinforce the action in a positive way.

CHAPTER 12

Changing beliefs? That's easy

Let me talk about beliefs again and make the point with another story. A group of frogs were hopping through the woods and two of them fell into a deep pit. All the other frogs gathered around the pit. When they saw how deep the pit was, they told their unfortunate friends they would never get out. The two frogs ignored these comments and tried to jump up out.

The other frogs kept telling them to stop, giving them the mournful message that they were as good as dead. Finally, one of the frogs took notice of what the other frogs were saying and simply gave up. He rolled over and died.

The other frog continued to jump as hard and as high as he could. Once again, the frogs poking their heads over the edge of the pit yelled at him to stop the pain and suffering and just die. He jumped with even more determination and finally made it out of the pit. When he emerged, the other frogs asked him: 'Why did you continue jumping? Didn't you hear us?'

The frog explained to them that he was deaf. He thought that when they were shouting at him they were encouraging him the entire time.

What you do depends largely on what you believe. Your beliefs are the most dominant, motivating or debilitating drivers you possess. As children many of us were told to try, try, try again when confronted with a particularly difficult task. If you really believe you can do something, you give yourself the opportunity to accomplish it. If you really believe you can't do something, you close down even the possibility of achievement. It doesn't matter how thin you slice it, there are always two sides.

Beliefs are so important in our activities. A belief is something that we feel with absolute certainty to be true. It is not necessarily true. It is enough that we feel that it is true. Your beliefs are your lenses to the perceptions that shape and colour your actions and ultimately your behaviour, and they are formed primarily from your feelings. The stronger your feelings, the more emotional intensity they contain and the stronger your belief. This process is vital if you aim to stop smoking.

You must believe that you can do it.

Beliefs are formed from three areas:

- From your direct experience.
- From your programming, that is, what you absorb directly from your peers and family.
- From external influences, such as thought viruses from media and from your surroundings.

The peak performance guru Tony Robbins says: 'Most of our beliefs are generalisations about our past based on our interpretations of painful and pleasurable experiences. Once accepted, our beliefs become unquestioning commands to our nervous system and they have the power to expand or destroy the possibilities of our present and future.' Clearly, Robbins goes big on beliefs as influences in our personality.

Beliefs, whether they are true or not, lie on a scale and vary on a continuum from an idea at the lower of your belief scale to a conviction at the highest level. When you have emotional intensity linked to an idea this powers up the belief to become a conviction.

From idea to belief to conviction

There are many examples of the power of beliefs to determine deeds, and sometimes revolutionary actions. At the beginning of the 20th century suffragettes chained themselves to the railings of Buckingham Palace because their beliefs were at the highest level. Their beliefs were a conviction. Their case was that women should have the right to vote. That conviction led to many kinds of action, some of which led to the other type of conviction – criminal conviction. Nevertheless, the strength of the belief did its job and women eventually had the vote.

In today's society conservationists chain themselves to trees demonstrating their conviction that it is essential to protect the environment. Think back too to the Aldermaston hikes at the height of anti-bomb activity in Britain. People marched to demonstrate their beliefs and convictions and have marched for scores of other causes before and since. However, do not assume that an individual who marches for one cause would march for every cause. The multi-cause marcher, in fact, is an extremely rare animal. He may not believe in the reasons for the other causes – and even if he believes in the reasons his belief could be at the lower end of the belief scale. To him they may be only ideas and may not have enough emotional intensity attached to them for him to act.

Empowering or limiting?

People, however, cannot easily be fitted into neat categories. Most people are mixtures, sometimes baffling mixtures, and many influences are constantly at work on them. Because of this human melange there is no such thing as a negative or a positive personality. The final choice of how you regard the world around you, your view of what you can and cannot do, and the beliefs you hold that shrink or expand your world are changeable. In line with these changes, beliefs can and do change. This fluid state is something that makes life and human nature interesting and makes positive change possible.

The changes that take place in beliefs and views are actually quite fascinating. There was a time when people believed that the world was flat and warned that if you sailed out to sea far enough you would fall off the edge. If anybody told you this today you would laugh your socks off. As it happens the Flat Earth Society still exists, and the astronomer Sir Patrick Moore, who obviously does not swallow this theory, believes there is a place for eccentric alternative thinkers such as flat earthers.

In 1959 Burt Reynolds and Clint Eastwood were both told at the same time by an executive of Universal Pictures that they would never succeed as actors. The Universal executive told Reynolds: 'You have no talent.' Then he told Eastwood: 'You have a chip on your tooth, your Adam's apple protrudes too far and you speak too slowly.' Those were the Universal man's beliefs at the time. Perhaps you are thinking: 'Enough said!'

Athletics sports are full of these surprises. The most celebrated event of recent history must have been Roger Bannister's record run in May 1954. Bannister, now Sir Roger, achieved the four-minute mile, which everybody had believed impossible. Luckily, Bannister did not give up on the idea. Something amazing happened after Bannister had registered his 3 min 59.4 sec. Within one year 37 other athletes had run the mile in less than four minutes. So what was that all about? Did these athletes suddenly become faster and train harder? No, the floodgates opened because Bannister had broken the psychological barrier and had shown what was possible. Athletes were no longer limited by this old belief. That's the important bit. Incidentally, the record at the time of writing is 3min 43.13sec, more than a quarter of a minute inside the so-called impossible four-minute time.

What about this for a belief? When you capture a wild horse and place it in a corral you can keep it there by erecting a fence containing a thin electric wire that carries a low current of electricity. The horse tries to escape but every time it touches the fence it suffers a small electrical zap. Whenever the horse brushes against the fence it gets the zap. It soon learns to look but not to attempt to escape. After a while the electricity can be switched off and the horse does not try to escape. Human ingenuity makes certain that the horse remains captured by a thought, a belief that it is a prisoner and that it is impossible to escape.

Limiting beliefs are not confined to the weak. An adult elephant is between 9ft and 13ft tall and weighs between 9,000lb and 13,000lb. You would think that very little would stand in its way. In his book *The Elephant and the Twig* Geoff Thompson tells the story of the elephant's limiting belief: 'In India they train obedience in young elephants (to stop them from escaping) by tying them to a huge immovable object, like a tree, when they are still very young. The tree is so large that no matter how hard the baby elephant pulls and tugs it cannot break free. This develops what is known as 'learned helplessness' in the creature. After trying so hard and for so long to break the hold, only to be unsuccessful again and again, it eventually believes that, no matter what it does, it cannot escape. Ultimately, as a fully grown adult weighing several tons, they can tie it to a twig and it won't escape. In fact, it won't even try.'

Limiting beliefs are invisible barriers created by the mind. That has a negative aspect to it. In this book the emphasis is on the positive. The good news is that your mind can also create empowering beliefs.

Think of all that you have been told about the bumble bee. People have always said that it is aerodynamically impossible for a bumble bee to fly, but thank heavens nobody told the creature itself. Luckily, it doesn't study the scientific principles that humans have discovered. It would have given up centuries ago. I don't know how the bumble bee thinks and what it sees as a problem, but it certainly believes it can fly, even though it has such a small wing span in relation to the weight of its body. The bumble bee's conviction that it can fly is so strong that it moves its wings at an incredibly fast rate, clocking up 200 beats a second. That speed is ten or 20 times the firing rate of the nervous system. It vibrates its wings like a rubber band. A nerve impulse shoots along and twangs the muscle, as if it is plucking a guitar string. This vibrates the wing up and down a few times before the next impulse is received. The bumble bee's belief is so strong that it has found a way to fly.

Dr Richard Bandler, the originator of neuro-linguistic programming, says: 'Behaviour is organised around beliefs. As long as you can fit a behaviour into someone's belief system, you can get him to do anything, or stop him from doing anything. A belief tends to be much more universal and categorical than an understanding. When you already have a belief there's no room for a new one unless you challenge and weaken the old belief first.'

CHALLENGING YOUR LIMITING BELIEFS

1. What do you think or believe about stopping smoking that limits you in succeeding?

2. What would be a more empowering belief? What is the opposite of the limited belief you used to have?

3. Now you have that new empowering belief, what would be different?

Complete this exercise for at least 3 beliefs before reading on. And use this exercise again as more beliefs you hold become apparent to your as you move forwards.

What have you missed

A friend of mine called Michael Neil wrote the book *You Can Have What You Want*. In it he tells this wonderful story of a man arriving in heaven.

One day, a human went to heaven in the way that humans often do. On arrival the human was greeted by a host of angels and given a tour of all heaven's wonders. During the viewing, the human noticed there was a room the angels quickly glided past every time they approached it.

'What's in that room?' the human asked.

The angels looked at one another uneasily as if they had been dreading the question. Finally, one of them stepped forward and said kindly: 'We're not allowed to keep you out, but please believe us – you don't want to go in there.'

The human's mind raced at the thought of what might be concealed in that room. What could be so horrible that all the angels of heaven would want to hide it away? The human knew that one should probably take angels at their word, but found it very hard to resist temptation. 'After all,' the human thought, 'I'm only human.'

Slowly walking towards the room, the human was filled with fear and wonder at what horrors might be about to be revealed. But, in fact, the room was filled with the most wonderful things imaginable – a beautiful home, beautiful objects, great wisdom, a happy family, loving friends and riches beyond measure.

Eyes wide, the human turned back to the angels and asked: 'But why didn't you want me to come in here? This room is filled with the most amazing things I've ever seen!'

The angels looked at one another sadly, then back at the human.
They told him: 'These are all the things you were meant to have while you were on earth, but you never believed you could have them.'

PRACTISING THE EMPOWERING BELIEF

1. Here is a great exercise for you. Firstly, what would you need to believe in order to know that you will stop smoking and never smoke again?

2. Now imagine that you really believe it.

3. What does that look like, feel like and sound like?

CHAPTER 14
Supercharge your motivation

I want to discuss reasons with you now. A reason is a justification for an action in support of a belief. You have to do some serious reasoning before you make your mind up and arrive at a belief. Think of your beliefs as a table top and your reasons to stop smoking are the table legs, all supporting the structure. If you have only one reason, it's like having only one leg to your table. The table will not then be secure, so it will wobble and easily topple over. The more legs you place under the table top, the stronger the table top support becomes.

However, you must have the reasons yourself. They will not magic themselves into existence and walk into your mind. Oprah Winfrey, the American television show hostess, puts the thought strongly, and the importance of the observation will become even clearer as we continue. She said: 'It doesn't matter who you are, where you come from. The ability to triumph begins with you. Always.'

It would be wise to remove as many reasons for smoking as you can and at the same time gather as many reasons as possible for stopping smoking. I know you must already have some reasons for stopping smoking and I know they are powerful reasons and there are many of them. If you had no reasons you wouldn't be reading this book now. I must repeat, however, that you have to produce the reasons, and what I am certainly not going to do is tell you all the reasons why *you* shouldn't smoke. I'm not going to tell you that smoking is bad for your health, that it causes cancer, that it obstructs your breathing or reduces your life expectancy. I'm not even going to tell you about the money you have wasted and continue to throw away. Right now I'm not going to tell you the reasons why you shouldn't smoke. You already know them, don't you? I have said before that I have never known smokers who thought smoking was actually good for them.

Moving away, moving towards

An important distinction is coming up. Decide whether your reasons are that you want to move away from something or move towards something. The distinction is not academic. It's vital if you are going to stop smoking.

Suppose I asked you: 'What are you looking forward to as an ex-smoker?' This is a crucial question and you should think hard about it. You might respond by telling me what you don't want, what you want to get rid of. Like most people, you hate the smell of stale tobacco on your clothes, or the after-taste in your mouth. Or perhaps you would say: 'I shouldn't smoke because it makes me short of breath when I'm walking or playing with my children.' All this is true, of course, but it will be little help in stopping your smoking habit.

Maybe you'll see the vital distinction if I tell you these reasons would be 'moving away from'. In effect, they are negative reasons for deciding to ditch the habit. On the other hand, you could say you are looking forward to clean-smelling clothes, or a nice fresh taste in your mouth, or that you must stop smoking because you will be fitter and breathe more freely when walking or playing with your children or grandchildren. I'd say: 'Now you're talking.' You would have 'moving towards' reasons. They are positive reasons.

Remember that I said you should devote some intense thought to your reasons for stopping. So let's look at how you go about it. When you're reasoning with yourself, you are searching for an answer, gathering a solution by considering possible options. As you put in the effort you should be focusing your mind on the 'moving towards' reasons for stopping smoking. You should be considering the benefits. It may sound somewhat crude but you should be asking: 'What's in it for me?'

There's such a lot worth living for, so it shouldn't be difficult to think up some of the benefits of being an ex-smoker. A few common reasons fall into the categories of health, wealth and friends and family. It may help you if we examine these a little more closely under the microscope.

Health: How is stopping smoking going to change your health? You might say that it will enable you to live longer, breathe more freely and have better skin. You might expect you would find it easier to walk up the stairs or uphill, or to jog or run – if you are into that sort of activity. It could mean that you would be able to play with the children for longer and kick a ball around with them. They are all positive reasons to stop smoking.

Wealth: How is stopping smoking going to change your wealth? We appreciate that extra money is not in itself a great motivator. What counts is what you do with the money, so you might say that it would buy you an extra holiday or a new car. The money may do something even more constructive for you. It could allow you to pay off your mortgage sooner or save for a deposit on a house. More commendable positive reasons to stop smoking.

Friends and family: How is stopping smoking going to change your friends and family? I would suggest that your children are less likely to start smoking if you don't smoke yourself. Your partner too is likely to be pleased about it.

Those are just a few of my thoughts. You will have your own thoughts on the subject. They may be quite different and they will be unique to you and your life and your reasons for stopping smoking. So how many more 'moving towards' or 'positive' reasons can you come up with when you really put your mind to it?

This, naturally, will demand a little work from you, but you are reading this book because you want to stop smoking. On the next page write down all your reasons. I can't step inside your head and discover what stopping smoking will mean to you, but I'm sure you know, so think up as many reasons as you can. It really doesn't matter how small or big they seem right now. The best idea is to get as many legs under your table top as possible. Just get that done and we'll refine them later.

Perhaps you can appreciate better now why Oprah Winfrey said it had to begin with you, the individual.

WHAT'S IN IT FOR YOU?
LIST ALL YOUR PERSONAL POSITIVE REASONS FOR STOPPING SMOKING

Now ask how important every reason is to you. How much value do you place on your reason? Return to your list of reasons and ask yourself the following questions:

- Why do you want to do it?
- Why is it important to you?
- How important to you is it?
- What are you prepared to do to get it?
- What would happen if you achieved it?

Next, grade your reasons, making a score of ten the highest and one the lowest.

Orr's law: In the mind

There is another way to look at this. Orr's Law derives from the model produced by the thinker and prover Dr Leonard Orr. It describes how reasons, values and belief patterns are acted on by the thinker and prover model in your mind. This model suggests that your reasons for doing or not doing something are fed into your beliefs and with a click and a whirr your thinker and prover are activated. In effect, whatever the thinker thinks the prover proves.

The thinker works on infinite possibilities and can think any thought you choose. The prover's task is much simpler as it operates on only one law. It supports the thinker by supplying evidence to substantiate the thinker's thoughts. It sorts all information, past, present and even future, to validate the thinker. Its action is rather like gathering evidence to build a case to be presented in court.

Let me give you a practical example as that sounds rather dry. If you think you can pass your driving test, your prover could support that thought with experiences in which you have previously succeeded at a task you set yourself. The prover could support the thinker by making comparisons with other people you know who have passed their driving test. Then you start to think: 'I'm bound to pass because I am just as competent a driver as they are.' In this case the prover gives you the reassurance and confidence you want as you go to that forbidding test centre.

If, on the other hand, you descend into a pessimistic state of mind and think you can't pass your driving test, your prover ferrets about for some negative data. It could provide you with alternative substantiation that reminds you of an article you may have read showing how driving tests are becoming more difficult. It could project you into the future so that you picture yourself messing up your three-point turn, or driving too quickly or too close to the car in front. The prover could compare you with drivers who have failed their tests and perhaps prove to you that you will fail too. The prover is hardly on your team if you look on the black side of everything. The sole purpose of the prover is to prove the thinker right.

This mental mechanism can therefore be a friend or an enemy. You know there have been times in your life when you really believed you could or could not do something. You had enough emotional intensity and reasons and your thinker thought positively or negatively. When you thought you could do something, such as passing your driving test, your prover went into action gathering information to support this thought, and, voilà, you achieved your goal.

The process is quite a powerful one and can be part of your mental armoury. Do you want your thinker to work for you? If you do, the prover will prove whatever you think.

It's a process that can be called up in any circumstances. Take the fat chap who wants to lose weight. It's Saturday evening and he's slumped on the couch at home watching television. The house is warm, the couch is wonderfully comfortable and this chap's favourite show is just coming up. In this lulled state the thinker has a thought: 'I just can't stick to eating healthy foods. I fancy a packet of crisps.'

That's enough to activate the click and the whirr that fire up the prover to take action. As the couch potato salivates the prover validates his thought by providing him with evidence that he just can't stick to eating healthily. The damage is done. Within a few minutes he is in front of the television with a packet of crisps, and the next day he can't understand why he gave in. It was all down to Orr's Law. The prover had given the thinker the data that permitted the overweight man to eat the unhealthy food. The prover had done its job, though admittedly it was a bad job.

The plump man needed to change his view of the packet of crisps. Consider it in a rather more vivid way. You are kissing the most attractive person in the world. What would that feel like? It would feel nice and pleasurable. Now what would it feel like if you kissed the world's ugliest, most hideous person? That would feel horrible, wouldn't it? It would be a painful experience, make no mistake! Yet the physical movement and action are the same. The difference is in how you perceive the event.

In a nutshell, when you change your thoughts, you change your feelings, which change your behaviour. So you must start changing your thoughts, feelings and emotions and you can start to associate enormous pleasure with stopping smoking and enormous pain with not stopping.

CHAPTER 15

Is it imagined or is it real?

Inside your head you are constantly at the mercy of deception and trickery. Your mind cannot tell the difference between imagination and reality. If a man had his eyes closed when he kissed a hideous woman he could have persuaded himself she was a stunning beauty. When you imagine something vividly your mind functions as if it were real. This trickery can happen when you are watching an emotionally moving film and you find you have to wipe a tear from your eye. In comedy shows the viewer grabs the whole box of tissues! Perhaps it's a scary movie, such as the classic *Psycho*, and it makes you jump out of your skin. It is reported that in the 1960s a cinemagoer even died in the audience of a heart attack while watching *Psycho*.

Your imagination can even alter your physical state. Suppose you are staying in a strange house and you suddenly hear something sinister downstairs. This is an experience we have all had, even in our own homes. That peculiar thing sounds like someone moving about. Your heart starts beating hard. It's thumping so much that you feel it could pop out of your chest. Your breathing increases to a panting rate. You listen carefully and then hear that noise again. What on earth could it be? You're convinced there's an intruder in the house. Despite your terror you grab a heavy object as if to defend yourself and you bravely wander down the stairs. Your hands are sweating, your heart is pumping, your breathing is accelerated. What sort of horror are you going to find? You creak open the kitchen door and find . . . nothing. You imagined the whole scene. In a second your whole body relaxes again, yet only a moment earlier it was working overtime, just because of a thought and because of your imagination. Don't feel embarrassed. You don't have to be a neurotic to hear sounds in the night.

The mind plays these tricks in all sorts of ways. They don't have to be frightening. I remember watching the former world motor racing champion Damon Hill in his Formula 1 car. It was a close-up shot of Hill swaying his head from side to side. I thought he must be careering along at 200mph. Then the camera panned back to show that Hill's car was stationary and he was waiting to begin the race. What Hill was doing was using his imagination. In his mind he was rehearsing vividly steering the correct racing line through every corner of the circuit. He was convincing himself that he was racing along, but he was also convincing me.

Harness your imagination

Imagine you had a good friend, or at least you thought he was a good friend. In fact, think of the best mate you ever had. You went everywhere together, and you did everything together. This experience gives you a comfortable feeling. Good friends are valuable because they can be trusted with confidences and will always help at times of need.

This was the type of friend you had and you were really close, or so you thought. Until the bombshell landed. Then you suddenly discovered he was a million miles from being a friend. In fact, in all those years he had been doing the worst possible things behind your back, telling lies about you, spreading gossip and breaking confidences. Not once, but over and over and over again.

How disillusioned and disappointed you were. Instead of being a friend he was an enemy all the time. Immediately you changed the way you thought about him and then you changed the way you behaved towards him. You really wouldn't want any more to do with him, would you?

The change was revolutionary and automatic. This is because the moment you change how you think about something, you change the way you feel about it. And if you change the way you feel about it, then you change the way you act. Think about it. If you have had an experience that shakes you rigid, doesn't it change how you behave in the future?

Now imagine that you have this experience with your smoking. You change the way you think about smoking, you change the way you feel about it, and you change the way you behave towards cigarettes. The biggest change is just around the corner. With changed attitudes you just don't want to smoke any more. However, bear in mind that all this is in your hands. Your mind can work for you or against you, depending on the information you give it to process.

MY SOLEMN AND BINDING PROMISE TO ME

I [name]
do solemnly declare that I will stop smoking.

In return for the (your reasons) _____

_____

_____

_____

benefits that are now within my reach permanently, with the best of my ability
I undertake to:

Read this book with care and understanding

Follow every instruction to the letter

Complete every simple exercise

Become a permanent ex-smoker

Signed _____

Dated _____

Complete this page and read it every day as you journey towards your target of
being a happy ex-smoker. It will remind you of your promise and commitment
and that will help you to keep on track

The power of words

What are words? We talk to ourselves and to others with words, but what are words? They are characters strung together to form labels that we attach to our experiences and to which we give references. Words give volume to our experiences. We give words life and meaning according to the emotional intensity of the value we place on an experience. However, look at words coldly. They are just symbols. A word that means one thing to you can have a different meaning for somebody else. The meaning of the word depends on the experience and references you attach to it. You know that certain words are like hot buttons, and they can be destructive or empowering. Although they are just symbols, they are another window to your feelings. They can clip your wings or help you to fly. There is the interesting quotation that angels fly because they take themselves lightly.

Even though they are only symbols, words can pack a punch. When we change an actual word, or even reframe the context, we change the meaning, the emotional intensity and the value we place on the response. So, by you simply choosing to change the words that you use, you can easily move from a weak and disempowering vocabulary to a strong and empowering vocabulary.

What, for example, does the word 'Varkis' mean to you? Right now it probably means nothing, because I made it up. However, what would Varkis mean to you if you heard it while having certain experiences? Imagine the references you would give it if your favourite footballer scored the magical winning goal a minute before time and shouted: 'Varkis!' Maybe you're watching the news and a lottery winner who has just picked up £5 million shouts: 'Varkis!' Depending on what the word symbol represents, you would have some experiences and references to underpin your meaning of the word Varkis.

In actual fact, I have discovered since I 'invented' the word that Varkis is a Latvian surname! If, therefore, you knew a Mr Varkis his face would flash into your mind when you heard the word.

Changing the meaning

What do the following words mean to you?

Love
Passion
Desire
Anger
Hate

These words, all familiar to you and in common usage, are powerful because the experiences and references you attach to them magnify the emotional intensity that you feel when you hear them. This pushes the emotional intensity higher still. Now think about the following phrases.

'I can't' implies that you have little or no control, and your mind registers this as weakening.

'I should' implies you have an obligation, without any firm commitment.

'I could' begins to open up opportunity and the potential of choice.

'It's not my fault' shows lack of responsibility, giving away control to someone or something else.

'I will' shows commitment to action in line with the goal.

And how do things change when you alter the word? What happens when you replace 'unable' with 'challenging', or 'fear' with 'excitement'? And how about 'failure' with 'learning experience'?

They are all words or symbols, but they can be clothed with the meanings you want them to have.

Voices in your head

Your internal dialogue is the voice chattering away to you in the back of your mind. It is intense and it goes at breakneck speed. As a result you can become lost amid that frantic talk. In its rapid deliberations it can say: 'I agree with what that fellow said.' It can tell you: 'That woman was nice.' Or it shouts: 'Ouch! My leg hurts.'

With this silent chatter going on inside the head it's no surprise that we talk to ourselves. After all, do you realise we learnt to do it at an early age? When you learnt to read and you read out loud you vocalised. A little later you were told to read to yourself; to read quietly; to read inside your head, and you sub-vocalised. In your head you said the words to yourself and you practised talking to yourself. Your mind rambled on with these random thoughts sending you messages. Repeated often enough this process becomes a mental tape loop and a self-fulfilling prophecy. Through every waking hour, you never stop saying things to yourself and your internal dialogue triggers physiological changes and a physical reaction results. From every thought you have this reaction can be positive or negative. But you can choose how you talk to yourself, can't you? It's you talking to you and you can say anything you want to.

QUIETENING YOUR INTERNAL DIALOGUE

1. To stop your internal chatter, stick out your tongue.

2. Take hold of the tip of your tongue between your finger and thumb.

3. Just listen.

4. Notice how that internal chatter just stops.

5. Whenever you want to stop your internal chatter, do this exercise.

CHANGING YOUR INTERNAL DIALOGUE

1. Choose a negative internal dialogue that you want to change, one in which you tell yourself: 'I just can't do it.' Or maybe: 'I want a cigarette.'

2. When you say those words to yourself how does it make you feel?

3. Okay, now change the voice to a high-pitched whine, the kind of voice you could never take seriously, and then repeat the dialogue.

4. What do you notice that is different about that? How does it make you feel?

No, no, no!

Your mind does not understand negation. But first, let me explain what negation is. You have probably already tried telling yourself not to smoke, saying to yourself such words as 'I am *not* going to smoke' or 'I *don't want* a cigarette'. Despite all this advice to yourself, you end up reaching for a cigarette. This is because you must have first already have thought about having a cigarette before you tell yourself not to do it. Let's try an experiment.

Whatever you do, do not think about a pink elephant. That's right, just put that pink elephant out of your mind. Have you done that? I'll bet you thought about a pink elephant! It is impossible not to visualise the pink elephant. Fortunately, no harm befalls you if you think about that creature.

However when you say that you are not going to have a cigarette you must already have thought about lighting one up. It works this way. You think: 'I am *not* going to smoke.' Yet you must have thought of smoking first. This thought triggers the process. You then try to stop that thought by thinking: 'No, I won't.' But your mind will already have sent a message to your body triggering all your feelings and emotions and automatic responses about 'smoking' before you post the message not to smoke. The thinking must be right to start with. And whatever you do, your mind cannot 'not think' about something.

CHAPTER 16
Focus Before Action

There is an old saying that where your focus goes action flows. You clearly get more of whatever you focus on. Not long ago I bought a new car, a resplendent new Mercedes four-wheel drive. I had had the car only three days when somebody shunted me. I was taking my children to school and sitting stationary in the traffic when a van drove straight into me, scratching the rear of my car. Maybe it was nasty of me but what made me feel better at the time was that the front of the van was completely bashed in. I suppose it's human nature, but it is funny that knowing the van was in a worse condition than my car gave me a warm feeling!

Anyway, my insurance company was incredibly efficient and helpful. Those considerate insurers arranged to have my car picked up and taken to a local garage to be fixed. Then they offered a hire car while the repairs were being carried out. They gave me a four-wheel drive as they agree in the contract to lend you an equivalent vehicle. However, they didn't have any Mercedes cars in stock at the time. Not to worry, they gave me a VW Touareg, a car I had not seen before. When my children saw it they asked what it was as they too had not seen one before. Not to worry again, as the car quickly found favour with them.

The next day I drove my children to school in the Touareg and my daughter piped up: 'Look, Dad, there's a red one.' Indeed, a red Touareg was passing by. A few minutes later my son said: 'Dad, there's a blue one.' So there was. I dropped off the children, and while driving back to my office I noticed a silver one. Now, the Touareg had been around for a few months at that time and clearly my children and I had seen them without actually noticing them.

However, as we were now using one, our focus of attention was directed towards Touaregs.

Have you ever had the experience of buying a new pair of shoes or a new mobile phone or a new watch, and all of a sudden you notice other people have the exact same thing, or the colour is the same? Your focus is creating action.

These instances illustrate another way your mind works on you. It provides a focus, which is very powerful.

Look at the next page. What do you see?

●

Well, what did you see?

You may have said it was a black dot or something similar, and you would be right, but the black dot compared with the white space is very small. However, you focused on the black dot, possibly to the exclusion of all the white space. What does this tell you about your smoking? Just as with your smoking when you become so focused on the problem, you noticed only the black dot and you missed all the white space. To control your focus ask yourself empowering questions. Whatever you look for you will find. With this knowledge, you should focus on being smoke-free as your solution.

This is not rocket science, merely a discipline. There is an apt anonymous quotation: 'The successful man is the average man, focused.'

This poem, called *A Small Boy*, by John Magliola, may help you:

> A small boy
> Looked at a star
> And began to weep.
> And
> The star said:
> 'Boy,
> Why are you weeping?'
> And
> The boy said:
> 'You are so far away
> I will never be able
> To touch you.'
> And
> The star answered:
> 'Boy,
> If I were not already
> In your heart
> You would not be able
> To see me.'

The state you're in

Your state is the mental, emotional and physiological condition that you are in. Your state affects your beliefs, values, reasons and capabilities. Think of an occasion when you went to an event with a friend. When you came away it seems that you had different experiences, though you had been sitting side by side and watched the same thing.

This sometimes happens when a critic reviews a film. The cinemagoer reads the crit and asks: 'Did we see the same film?' The two people definitely saw the same film but had totally different views of it. That's because the state you are in at any moment determines your perceptions of reality, and also affects your decisions and behaviours. Your decisions and behaviours are not equal to your capabilities. Instead, they are equal to the state you are in at that particular moment, and thus they can be very different in another state.

Listen for that word 'state' in casual conversation, maybe at the supermarket or in the bus queue. You've often heard somebody say: 'Look at the state of him.' Or somebody flustered might say: 'I'm in a right state today.' We see something and we respond by going into a state, which can often be a resourceful state and lead to positive behaviour. The opposite is an unresourceful and limiting state, which can lead to negative behaviour. If you want to communicate, act and respond in the best way to yourself and others you have to submerge yourself in the right state. Often this will involve shutting out negative external influences.

Let me explain desirable and undesirable states with a simple story. You wake up one morning and open the curtains. My, it's a superb day with the sun shining down from the crystal clarity of a blue sky. Aren't you lucky! You have the day off and as you open the window and enjoy the fresh breeze you say: 'It's a great day.' In fact, you even feel like singing *Oh, What a Beautiful Morning*. You stroll down to the corner shop to buy the paper and as you pass people you smile and wish them a good morning. These equally contented people smile back, and that makes you smile even more. It gets better. You notice something glinting at you from the pavement and as you draw nearer you see it's a £1 coin. You pick it up and say: 'It's going to be a great day.' Everything seems to go just right for the whole day.

Of course life isn't always so generous to you. When you wake up on the day in question and open the curtains it's snowing. The drive is under a thick layer of snow. As you open the window the fresh crispness hits you and you say: 'Typical. Snow on my day off. What an awful day.' There's none of that cheerfulness that filled you when the sun was shining. *Oh, What a Beautiful Morning* seems out of place. You trudge and stump through the snow to the corner shop to buy the paper keeping your eyes firmly fixed on the ground so that you don't have to acknowledge anyone. You seem to have gone off people. You would feel like cursing anybody who extended a cheerful greeting to you. Let's hope nobody tries selling you insurance this day. You're not nice to know. You notice something glinting in the snow and as you draw nearer you see it's a £1 coin. You pick it up and complain: 'Why couldn't it be a £5 note?' Nothing pleases you this morning. And for the whole day nothing seems to go right.

At the mercy of moods

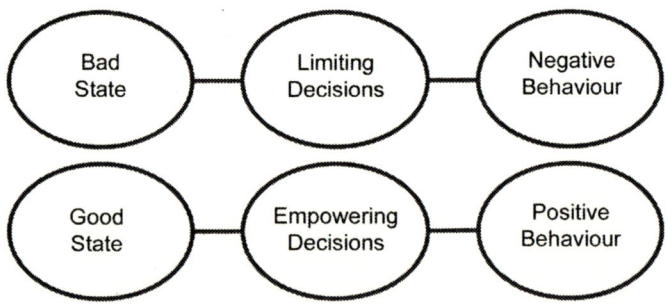

As you see, your state directly influences the way you do everything. That day had dawned with the same potential, snow or shine, but you reacted positively or negatively depending on the weather. You were grouchy even when you found a £1 coin. When you learn how to access your most resourceful state, you create empowering decisions. Your mind and body are inextricably linked and your movements can instantly change how you feel. They can literally change your state.

There's a little exercise you can perform if you want to test this statement. Try it, preferably in private because it is somewhat unorthodox and somebody sensitive could feel a ninny with an audience. Stand up straight, look at the ceiling and shout out: 'Yes, yes, yes!' I know it may seem a little strange but do it anyway You can even have a little chuckle to yourself as you do this, but just notice what happens. I'm sure you'll start to feel different. By doing something positive – nothing's more positive than yes – you will actually be changing your state. You won't feel so shy about this routine now. Do it five times and see how much you can improve your state just by moving your body.

CHAPTER 17

Conscious and unconscious

Now get on familiar terms with that wonderful machine inside your head. First, there is your conscious mind, which is everything of which you are aware right now. In 1956 Dr George A. Miller wrote a paper called *The Magical Number Seven, Plus or Minus Two*. Miller's research showed that the conscious mind has the capacity to be aware of between five and nine items of information at any one time.

Test his theory. Start by becoming aware of your feet, look at every individual toe. Now listen to the sounds in the room. What can you hear? Maybe there's nothing, but even if it's the sound of silence concentrate on it. Then turn your attention to your hand. Notice the feeling of a ring on your finger or a watch on your wrist. Become aware of the weight of the watch as well as the feel of it. Next, become aware of the temperature of the room, notice the rise and fall of your chest as you breathe. You started with your feet, didn't you? What happened to them? You have probably forgotten about your feet and your toes and that was after only six pieces of new information. This is because your conscious mind screens out all that is unimportant to you at any moment.

Sigmund Freud, the father of psychoanalysis, likened the mind to an iceberg. The small tip of the iceberg is the conscious mind and the huge part below the surface is the unconscious mind. Your conscious mind works on whatever you are pointing it at. You have your own evidence of the way it operates if you are in a busy bar or restaurant, going 19 to the dozen in an interesting conversation. You are so consciously focused on that conversation and so intent on listening to the friend to whom you are talking that all the other sounds fade into the background. You listen, you hear and you absorb information. Your conscious mind is that part of you in which most of your learning begins.

Now for the vast area below the tip of Freud's iceberg. Your unconscious mind is that vast warehouse or database of information. You are generally unaware of it but everything you have ever learnt or experienced is stored away in the back of your mind, the unconscious part. What this contains is like a movie of your life. If I asked you what you were doing last Christmas you would have to raid this warehouse. Where you were? Who was with you? And what happened? It is unlikely that you were thinking of last Christmas moments ago, but now that I have brought your attention to it your unconscious can rifle through your records and provide you with the content. The images of the Christmas tree all lit up, the party with the neighbours and poor drunken Uncle Harry having to be carried into bed flash into your consciousness.

All your learning, including the skills and abilities from your conscious mind and even the genetically predisposed learning passed down to you through your DNA, is warehoused in your unconscious mind. It is an ultra mega library, comparable to the internet but more efficient. It is constantly running in the background, and your whole autonomic nervous system, including your breathing and the beating of your heart, is run via your unconscious. This part of your mind even regulates your core body temperature to within a one degree Centigrade – a little over or under this and you become ill.

The habit you learnt

Have you ever thought that smoking was a learned process? It had to be, and you did a great job teaching yourself. You weren't born a smoker, and for whatever reason at some time in your life you decided to try smoking. This entailed quite a bit of learning. You had to learn how to inhale, you had to learn how to exhale, you had to learn how to hold a cigarette, you had to learn how many cigarettes to smoke in a day. All this took practice. Most people don't even like their first few cigarettes, and you probably didn't. Perhaps they made you feel dizzy or nauseous. This was your body's system screaming at you: 'Danger!' For some reason you took no notice and carried on. You continued to smoke and persevered with the habit and eventually you became a smoker.

You made progress as a smoker and continued learning. You began to do other things in your life and you created associations. Other habits developed and there were smoking triggers. You learnt to light up after a meal or with a drink or during a break at work. You learnt to do this with your smoking until eventually it became automatic. It was second nature to pull out a cigarette if you did certain things. Do you believe now that you had to learn to smoke, with all its behaviour patterns?

The unconscious travels to the conscious

The human mind is a near-perfect learning machine. It is automatically wired to store learnt processes and it's a multi-purpose tool. The proof of this assertion is that there are literally millions of things that you once had to learn to do that you now perform automatically without having to think about them.

That learning process is fascinating in itself. When you first learnt something, the learning was conscious and you really had to concentrate. You had to practise. Remember how you took the wheel of a car for the first time. You had to learn how to use the clutch and accelerator properly, how to get to the biting point and to control the acceleration. You had to learn the mirror and indicator disciplines, and how to change gears. After a time your driving became automatic, and today you can drive without having to think about all those things. This is because as soon as you had learnt these exercises they were filed away in your unconscious mind in the place where you keep all learnt processes. A vault was built around them to protect them and to make sure that you didn't forget how to drive. With this information packed away neatly in the big unconscious department, you could free your conscious mind so that you could think about something else.

The millions of things that you once learnt consciously to do and which you now do unconsciously and automatically include tying your shoelaces, swimming, walking and perhaps riding a bicycle. After you had learnt to do those things they were stored, like driving a car, in the unconscious part of your mind and protected by that virtual fortress, ensuring that they were a part of you. There is no thinking about them, no forgetting them.

Your mind is highly efficient and practical. After all, it wouldn't do to forget how to walk or swim. Imagine being in the middle of a swimming pool and suddenly forgetting how to swim, or talking to a shop assistant and suddenly forgetting how to talk. That kind of thing doesn't happen because learnt processes are stored and protected in your unconscious mind. There is one snag. There had to be, didn't there? Your unconscious doesn't distinguish between good and bad, or positive and negative. It stores and protects all learnt processes in the same way.

And as you know, you learnt how to smoke and how to hold a cigarette, how to inhale and how to exhale. You learnt how many cigarettes to smoke in a day. Just like the ability to drive, these learnt processes became stored in your unconscious mind so that you could smoke without thinking about it. These also become stored and protected in the vault that is your unconscious.

You added to this smoking knowledge too, didn't you? Along the way you made associations between your smoking and other circumstances, events or activities building up repetitive patterns in your everyday life. You may have always smoked with coffee and tea, while you were on the phone, during or after a meal, in the car, before a task, after a task, at certain times and with certain friends. As with everything else you had learnt, these became patterns of behaviour that were stored side by side with smoking in your unconscious mind. The result was that when you did X or Y you automatically had a cigarette without even thinking about it. There can be no doubt in your mind now that your smoking and whatever goes with it are learnt and ingrained in you.

How the mental traffic works

Equally, there can be no doubt that all this is going to change if you stop smoking. To change a learnt habit or response, now stored in your unconscious mind, you must let the solution unfold from within and you need to become consciously aware of it. You must make it conscious because when a habit becomes conscious once again, it is held in that thinking part of your mind. There you can control it and ultimately you can change, replace or delete it from your life if you so choose.

CALCULATING YOUR CIGARETTES

For the next 48 hours put a cross below every time you have a cigarette, then add up the total number of lines and divide by two. You will then have the average number of cigarettes that you smoke in a day. We will use this number a little later on.

For example

Day 1 – x x x x x x x x x x x x x x x x x x x x x x x x

Day 2 – x x x x x x x x x x x x x x x x x x x x

Total cigarettes in 48 hrs = 44 ÷ number of days (two) = 22 cigarettes

Average cigarettes per day = 22

Day 1 –

Day 2 –

Total cigarettes in 48 hrs = _____ ÷ number of days (two) = _____ cigarettes

Average cigarettes per day = _____

WHICH CIGARETTES SEEMED MORE OR LESS IMPORTANT TO YOU?

Why did they seem the most or least important?

Where were you?

Who were you with at the time?

What were you doing?

What were you thinking?

CHAPTER 18

The seven illusions of smoking

Let's look at smoking as an illusion, something that deceives the senses or mind by appearing to exist when it does not – or appearing to be one thing when it is, in fact, another. Do you doubt that your smoking is a mass of illusions? Illusions are a figment of your imagination and, unfortunately, as we have already established, your mind cannot distinguish between imagination and reality. Have you ever had the experience of sitting on a stationary train on the platform when another train on the track right next to you begins to move? You feel you are actually moving. You get the sensation even though you know your train is standing still.

Illusions are dogging us all the time. Imagine setting a task for two people. You tell the first that a valuable diamond ring has been lost in your garden and you say: 'I'll bet you can't find it before nightfall.' You tell the second one about the diamond ring and threaten him: 'If you don't find it before nightfall I'll chop off your right hand.' Because it's a mental problem the second person would be in a panic state and would be less likely to find the ring. It's this kind of situation that confuses smokers and, incidentally, non-smokers. They think that because smoking is killing them they should be able to stop. All that does is to give smokers a stronger desire to escape from the trap. However, what holds them in the trap is the illusion that they enjoy smoking or need to smoke, or that they will find it impossible to stop. The good news is that we are about to expose and dispel these illusions so that you can take another step forward.

Another little experiment to demonstrate the point. Look at the illusion of the spiral. It's a great test of the tricking of the mind. As you stare at it, it can become almost 3D, like a tunnel. Or perhaps it begins moving. You've been tricked because logically you know the image is completely flat.

This type of experience can be honed into a fine art. Think of those professionals who dazzle and entertain us with illusions. There once was a television programme called *Breaking the Magician's Code: Magic's Biggest Secrets Finally Revealed*. This really angered many magicians. A chap called the Masked Magician would show you how an illusion works. When you knew the secret it didn't have the same hold over you. It had lost all its power – no wonder the man's fellow magicians got upset!

Smoking is just like the magician's trick. You think smoking does a whole lot of things for you but it performs nothing more than a deception. You just think it does you all these favours and that's why I say it's an illusion. I want to look at these smoking illusions, seven in all.

ILLUSION ONE: WILLPOWER

Here's an old chestnut. Many smokers say: 'I can't stop. I just don't have any willpower.' Let me explain. Willpower, as most people understand it, is a psychological illusion, because it doesn't really exist. Willpower is just a nine-letter word to which you have attached high emotional value. Just analyse the word for what it is. Will is the faculty by which you decide on and initiate action, and power is the ability to do something. Now willpower looks a little different, doesn't it?

You merely deceive yourself with that word willpower. We use it as a label for something we have already predetermined is going to be difficult. There are things that you do because you enjoy them but other people say those things must take some willpower. Here's a personal example. Having lost four stone, I have exercised at the gym consistently four times a week for more than ten years. Before I take my children to school I spend up to two hours working out every day. Perhaps people think I'm having to force myself. That idea couldn't be further from the truth. The working out has nothing to do with willpower. I do it because I really enjoy it. Think about something you really enjoy doing, so much that you look forward to doing it again and again. You'd laugh if somebody suggested willpower had to be summoned up for it. What keeps you doing it is the pleasure you associate with it. Apply this to the tobacco habit. When you change your feelings so that you really enjoy not smoking, you will enjoy that feeling so much that you will want to continue not smoking.

I'll turn the argument around. If willpower really did exist you would use it to continue smoking. It takes willpower to spend your money on cigarettes, because they don't magically appear in your hand. Go one pace backwards – it takes willpower to go out and buy them. When you've got them it takes willpower to light them, to inhale not once, not twice, but maybe more than ten times for every cigarette. Don't you think it takes willpower to have to inhale on a piece of paper filled with plant leaves and to breathe it in anywhere from 50 to 300 times a day?

Even more, doesn't it take willpower to smoke when you know that it's harming your health and how much it's draining your finances? Doesn't it take willpower to resist people telling you to stop? It must be a strong will that keeps you smoking when you know all these things. You don't swallow all that surely?

Consider two men who desperately want the same unobtainable thing. One is strong-willed, the other has no willpower. The first maintains silence, the other is constantly agitated. Yet the will-power plays no part in obtaining the unobtainable.

However, it is willpower that you use when the two parts of your mind are in conflict between the angel and the devil. When you change the way you think and feel the whole of your mind is pointed in one direction, you have no need to battle with your wills.

Strong man Philip

Philip's story makes the willpower point strongly. He was a 20-a-day smoker with an impressive background. He was a member of the elite SAS, just about the toughest and most determined unit in the army. SAS men are trained to survive in any climate, and Philip spent more than ten years serving in some of the most dangerous and hostile terrains and conditions one could ever imagine. The worst befell him when he was captured during the Gulf War behind enemy lines. He was physically and psychologically tortured by his captors to obtain information, but his willpower was so strong that even under this immense pressure he did not disclose any information to the enemy. Such determined people are few and far between.

Nor was this stern example a one-off. Philip's willpower was so strong that every year he would push himself through one of the original endurance tests for SAS selection. This was a 40-mile march across the Brecon Beacons that had to be completed in less than 20 hours with a load of more than 55lb, plus water, food and a rifle. There was no doubting that Philip was a man with an iron will. However, it would have been a shock to most people to hear this giant of a man at 6ft 2in with a powerful physique explaining he lacked the willpower to stop smoking. But, of course, he had missed the point. Philip certainly had willpower by the bucketful. All he had not done was to change the way he thought about smoking.

ILLUSION TWO: SMOKING RELAXES YOU

We come to another of the old chestnuts. Some smokers claim to find smoking helps them to de-stress, to relax, or to concentrate, or maybe all three. They are the victims of a big illusion.

Be honest about those occasions when you have lit up to combat stress. Smoking when you are stressed is an automatic response to a specific condition and in the long run it is no help. I remember one Christmas when I was at my cousin's house. The neighbours had done the usual Christmas thing and had dropped in for the annual glass of sherry. The telephone rang and my cousin was given the message that a close friend of his had just died. On hearing the sad news one of the neighbours offered my cousin a cigarette. Maybe this would not normally seem strange, but the neighbour actually knew my cousin had stopped smoking ten years earlier. He was one of the first people I helped to stop.

This was the myth acted out in front of me. The neighbour had the automatic response that in stressful times and situations my cousin smoked and that a few puffs somehow helped. I may sound harsh if I ask whether the cigarette would bring the friend back to life. Would smoking stop my cousin grieving? Would smoking change anything? So then I ask why the neighbour would even think that smoking would help in this stressful situation? Quite simply, he had fallen victim to the illusion that cigarettes calm people when they are stressed.

The unpalatable truth is that the feeling of stress is caused by the last cigarette you smoked. The science of it is, when you inhale a cigarette the powerful drug nicotine hits your brain within seven seconds and your nicotine levels rise. So the nicotine has an effect within a very short space of time, and of course, when the levels have risen there is only one place they can go. You've guessed it – they start to go down after a while. Your drug levels dive lower and lower still until you start to feel edgy, irritable, maybe anxious.

What do you do? You reach for another cigarette and within seven seconds the nicotine hits your brain and your drug levels rise again. You feel relaxed but you have been sucked into a vicious circle. This is addiction because you are topping up your drug levels to get your usual high. The deception is being perpetuated. You repeat this exercise over and over again and the illusion becomes stronger. You really think those cigarettes are helping you to relax.

Back to that bad news at Christmas. The smoker who experiences the physical anxiety from a real-life stressful moment, such as my cousin's bereavement, automatically thinks: 'I know, when I have felt stressed before I've had a cigarette, and the cigarette took away the stress.' However, that is such a dangerous illusion. The smoking was the very thing that caused the anxiety in the first place. Light up again at your peril because the next cigarette makes certain that you will feel the anxiety again. When the anxiety bites at you again you simply top up the drug levels. The whole cycle is insidious. The smoker is so wrapped up in the emotions of the stress of a bereavement, or a personal crisis, he is not even aware that smoking didn't help the last time. Therefore, the smoking and the illusion go on.

If you feel cigarettes relieve stress, answer this. Before you started the habit did you feel stressed 20, 30 or 40 times a day? Of course not, and that says it all. So let's not kid ourselves any more. It's actually impossible that cigarettes can calm you or relax you as nicotine itself is a stimulant. In physical health terms smoking goes for the heart and makes it work harder. A smoker's heart can beat up to 10,000 times a day more often than a non-smoker's to compensate for reduced oxygen levels. You can liken this to a car engine running at the traffic lights with the driver's foot on the accelerator.

So if smoking just feeds the stress, how can you claim that it relaxes you? Look closely at this illusion. Have you ever noticed that you actually smoke more on holiday?

The scene is of you lying on a sun lounger and enjoying the warm sunshine, the break from work, the absence of everyday tasks. There's nothing to disturb you. You are looking lazily over a long golden sandy beach, but just what are you doing? You're actually smoking more! I know that whenever I was on holiday in my smoking days I tended to smoke more heavily. But hang on – wasn't I already relaxed? Of course I was. Doesn't that sound daft? If smoking helped me to relax why was I smoking more when I was

THE SMOKING CYCLE

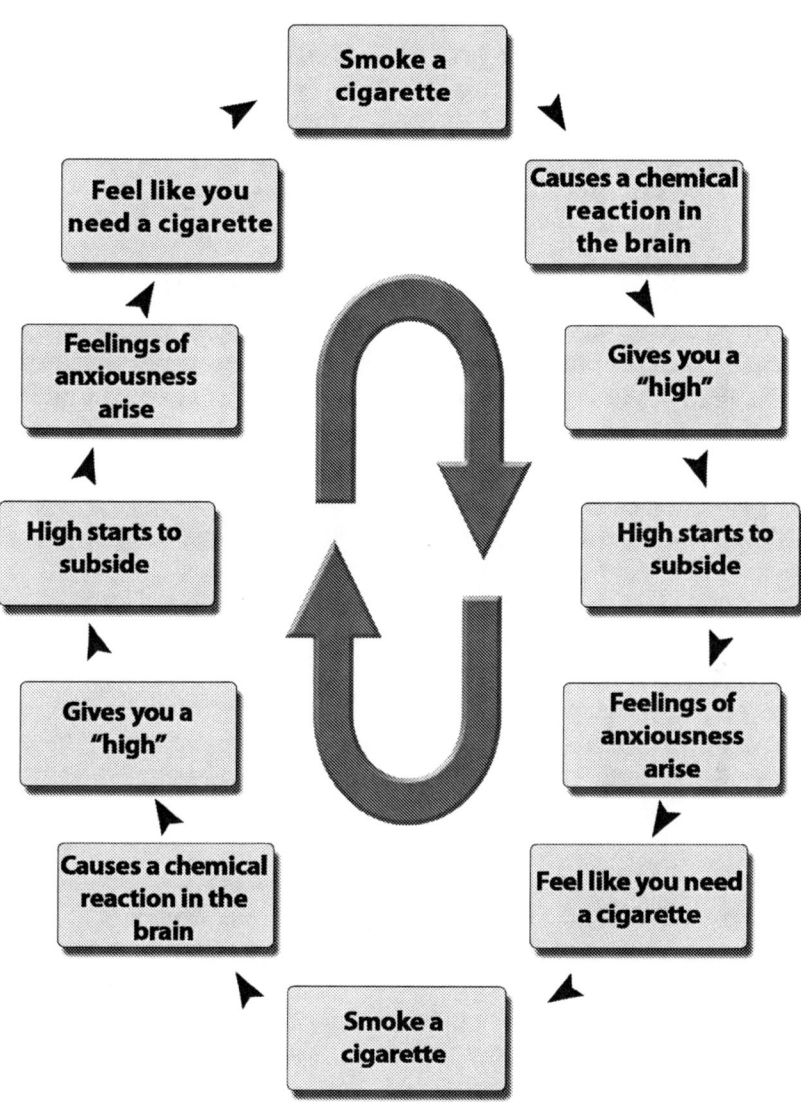

already relaxed? The simple answer is that smoking creates the illusion that it helps you to relax. Another myth is exploded.

Look at the flip side of saying that a cigarette relaxes you. If this is the case it follows that you were unrelaxed before you had a cigarette. Don't delude yourself further. The 20-a-day man is not unrelaxed 20 times a day. However, if he is, smoking won't solve the problem anyway, so why bother smoking? It's as useful as putting a plaster on your hand to cure a headache.

ILLUSION THREE: YOU ENJOY SMOKING

Oh, the self-kidding. This illusion really tickles me, yet thousands of smokers profess the pleasure they get from cigarettes. I remember Stephanie coming to see me and saying: 'You have been highly recommended and I know lots of smokers that you have helped to stop smoking. But I'm different. I enjoy smoking.'

Stephanie was a typical 20-a-day smoker and I wanted her to appreciate what she had just said. So I asked Stephanie to forget about smoking for a moment. Then I posed a question: 'What do you enjoy doing in life?' I told her to take a little time to think of something she really loved. She replied: 'I enjoy eating out.' So what was it about eating out that she enjoyed so much?

Stephanie gave me quite a collection of plus points: 'I enjoy the company. I enjoy not having to prepare the food. I enjoy having somebody else do the cooking. I enjoy the different flavours. I enjoy the aroma. I enjoy the taste. I enjoy not having to wash up.'

As she went through all these pleasurable experiences her whole physiology changed. Her body literally sat up and a big smile spread across her face. 'Excellent,' I said. 'And what do you enjoy about smoking?'

This blunt question was a conversation-stopper. She just looked at me blankly. 'I don't know,' she said. 'I just enjoy it.' I persisted: 'OK,' I said, 'but when you told me you enjoyed eating out and I asked you why, you reeled off a long list and told me in detail why you enjoyed eating out. Now I'm asking you what you enjoy about smoking and you seem lost for words.' I then landed her with this one: 'Could it be that you don't actually enjoy smoking, but because you do it 20 times a day you fool yourself into thinking you do actually enjoy it? It would be crazy to do something 20 times a day that you don't even enjoy.' I was not pulling any punches.

The reality is that the only enjoyment or pleasure is the restoration of the drug levels that were pumped in by the previous cigarette.

ILLUSION FOUR: SMOKING GIVES YOU CONFIDENCE

A woman called Susan provides me with the next illusion. Susan was a 40-a-day smoker and she said cigarettes gave her confidence. What ensued was like a game. It went like this.

'Do you mean you have no confidence?'
'Yes, that's right. Smoking gives me confidence. I have no confidence.'
'Are you sure that you have no confidence?'
'Yes, I'm sure.'
'Are you really sure you have no confidence?'
'Yes, I'm really sure I have no confidence.'
'Are you really, really sure you have no confidence?'
'Yes, I'm really, really sure I have no confidence.'
'So you're confident that you don't have any confidence. You're confident about that, yet you are not smoking now.'
She looked at me and said: 'That's right!'
'So it's not that you don't have confidence. Of course everyone has confidence. Everyone has a resource when they achieve something and they were confident about it. And there are things that you face on a daily basis and you're confident that you can do them, or you face situations you have to handle and you're confident that you can.'

That was the real point. Just think of some area in your life or something that you do where you are confident. You don't have to be smoking to feel that way, do you? Therefore, you are actually confident without smoking. Cigarettes do not give you confidence. They create an illusion that makes you think they give you confidence.

ILLUSION FIVE: SOMETHING TO DO WITH YOUR HANDS

Let's revisit that learning process. You taught yourself to smoke, for sure. If you are smoking and inhaling 20 cigarettes a day and you are moving your hand ten times for every cigarette smoked, you are making 200 additional hand movements in that day. This adds up to 73,000 additional hand movements a year. In other circumstances I might say it's good exercise! But you have programmed your hands to think they must be doing something, so you have learnt to do it.

However, think back to a time when you didn't smoke. What about that argument now? Without cigarettes in your life your hands didn't need to be doing anything. They were all right then, so what's happened? Your habit started and has persisted, so that your hands have forgotten about that time when they didn't have to accommodate a cigarette. Compare an adult with a cigarette to a child with a dummy. The child pushes the dummy into his mouth and sucks on it. When the dummy-sucking finishes the child is so used to doing something with his hands that he can often switch to thumb-sucking and even nail-biting. Then this all goes. The child learns to stop this hand-mouth action and, lo and behold, he doesn't have to be doing something with his hands.

Like everything else to do with smoking, holding the cigarette is a habit, and saying you need the cigarette to occupy your hands is self-deception once again. It's pretty ridiculous anyway, isn't it? If you want something in your hand, wouldn't a pencil do the job, instead of a dangerous burning weed?

ILLUSION SIX: IT'S A HABIT

Use this argument and you really are chicken. Smokers who say they can't stop because smoking is a habit are taking the easy option. Just blame the habit and you don't have to substantiate your reasoning. 'It's not my fault, it's just a habit,' say some smokers. There's hardly an easier option in the book.

A habit is something you have done over and over again. You condition yourself through regular repetitive practice until the action becomes second nature. Eventually you actually do it without thinking about it.

Remember Pavlov? The Russian physiologist famed for his study of conditioned reflexes showed that a habit can be formed and changed quickly. Pavlov would ring a bell whenever he fed a dog. After doing this a few times Pavlov observed that the dog salivated in response to the bell. Thus he had created a conditioned habit. Pavlov then changed the response. When he rang the bell the dog salivated as usual and trotted towards him for his food. However, instead of feeding the dog Pavlov gave him a small electric shock. A few shocks later the dog relearnt that the bell equalled pain and would instantly run away when he heard the ringing.

Apply this to your smoking habit. When you have more perceived pleasure to continuing your habit than the perceived pain to stopping it, you will continue. When you have more perceived pleasure to stopping your habit compared with the perceived pain of continuing it, you will stop. However, some habits are more damaging than the Pavlov dog's conditioned response. The theologian Nathaniel Emmons could well have had smoking in mind when he said: 'Habit is either the best of servants or the worst of masters.'

At this point let's try an experiment to show how habits can be changed. Fold your arms and notice which one you have on top. Open them out wide and fold them again. It's more than a racing certainty that you will have the same arm on top. Carry out that exercise again. When you fold your arms again the same one is on top, isn't it? The positioning is highly predictable because at some time in your life you formed a habit. When you fold your arms the same arm is on top every time.

Now for the interesting bit – especially interesting if you want to change your smoking habit. Unfold your arms, open them out wide and refold them with the opposite arm on top this time. How does that feel? You probably had to think about it and perhaps it feels a little strange. But if you want to change the way you fold arms you can do it. If you practised folding your arms the different way 10 or 20 times every day and continued practising it until it felt comfortable, you would soon form a new habit. It would then be comfortable to fold your arms with the new arm on top. This particular exercise may be pointless except that it shows you can form new habits.

Give habits some thought. You have developed lots of everyday habits, such as brushing your teeth. How many times do you brush your teeth every day? The number of times has become a habit. This habit, however, is one you have chosen to control, if you're a balanced human being. You don't feel the need to gallop out of work to brush your teeth, or keep toothpaste and a brush in your car just in case. You don't even panic on a night out that you may not have enough toothpaste to last until the morning.

But there are problematic habits. I read an article about a woman who lived with an abusive violent partner for more than 20 years. That's a long time to take punishment. When she was asked why she hadn't cleared out sooner she said: 'I stayed with him out of habit.' Now that is a strange habit. She was, therefore, asked why she finally left him. She said: 'There came a point where I couldn't bear the pain any more and the fear of staying was greater than the fear of leaving.' She added: 'When I finally broke that habit and left him, my life was so much better and this became a new habit.'

That is one uncomfortable habit but the woman did find a way to change it. Whether you know it or not, you are already familiar with changing habits. Think of your daily routine. Perhaps you wake up at 7am every day. That is a habit to which you have become accustomed and you do it automatically. You can even wake up before the alarm clock if you have conditioned your mind and body to become alert at a certain time. This may be because you have a busy schedule and early-morning time is particularly useful. You get peace and quiet, nobody telephones and nobody pesters you. Then you go on holiday for a fortnight. The routine should be quite different but for the first few days you still wake at 7am. However, there's no reason to leap out of bed at this time while you're on holiday, so you turn over and go back to sleep for a few more hours. A day or two later you no longer wake up at 7am. Then it's all change again! You come home and resume your daily routine and it's hard to wake at 7am. You have slipped out of the habit.

Some things appear disgusting to you, such as somebody picking his nose and eating it, and you wouldn't practise that to form a habit. Other things appear acceptable or even rewarding and you practise them to create a habit.

Julie developed a habit that took her over every evening. When the children had gone to bed and her husband was working nights, she plonked herself in front of the television with two packets of biscuits and a mug of tea. She was OK with that habit until she caught sight of herself in the mirror. Oh dear, she suddenly felt extremely unhappy about all the weight she had gained. It caused her considerable pain. In fact, it was like a blinding light because at that moment she made a decision and changed the things with which she associated pain and pleasure. She associated pain with wolfing down the biscuits and pleasure with good eating habits. It was a big change for her but she did this night after night until she conditioned herself to respond with a good habit.

Have I told you enough to convince you? The thought that you can't stop smoking because it's a habit is simply another nonsensical illusion that the cigarettes create, an illusion that you can sweep away. As these examples show, the easiest way to cancel out a bad habit is to replace it with a good one, and smokers can do this by associating severe pain with smoking and great pleasure with not smoking. Follow this exercise until not smoking becomes your new habit.

A little soundbite might help: Motivation is what gets you started, habit is what keeps you going.

As we have already learnt, a habit is a pattern of behaviour. If you break the pattern you break the behaviour. The old vinyl records give us a good comparison. These records worked through the pattern on the vinyl. If you took the needle off the record player and continually scratched the record back and forth, then the music would never be the same again. The pattern would have been broken for ever.

Stickability plays a big part in this too. To form a new habit you must regularly and persistently practise a new pattern, and condition it to become part of you. If you wanted to become fitter you wouldn't go to an aerobics class once and say: 'OK, I'm fit now.' That would be ridiculous. Apply the same principle if you decide to stop smoking. I remember reading about a celebrated pianist, who said: 'If I don't practise for one day I notice. If I don't practise for two days my critics notice. And if I don't practise for three days my audience notices.'

Be vigilant for those actions that trigger lighting up – a meal, a cup of tea, driving, drinking alcohol and killing time while waiting.

The king's lesson

There is the story of a king who would hold a lavish banquet every year and invite the most important people from his lands. The king sent for his finest soldiers and ordered them to all the corners of his realm, scouring the country in search of wonderful performers.

On the evening of the banquet a great magician was entertaining. He was brilliant and he captivated the king and all the royal guests with his skill. At the end of his performance the king said: 'What a gift this man has, a God-given talent.' The king's wise counsellor turned to his monarch and said: 'My lord, genius is made, not born. This magician has mastered his skill through repetition and practice.'

The king turned in anger to the wise counsellor as he questioned his word and challenged his belief. The king was so irate that he summoned his guards and told them: 'Throw this man into the dungeon, and as he has the manners of a pig, give him two piglets for cellmates.'

From the very first day the counsellor arrived in his cell, he took hold of the piglets, one under each arm, and marched up and down his cell, and up and down the stairs to the cell door. He continued this day after day, week after week, month after month. As the piglets became older they grew in size and weight, and every day with repetition and practice the wise counsellor grew in strength and size.

After many months the king remembered his counsellor, wondering whether he had learnt his lesson. With a snap of his fingers the king instructed the guards to bring the counsellor before him.

When the prisoner appeared, he had become a man of powerful physique, carrying a huge pig under each arm. As he stood there the king exclaimed: 'What a gift this man has, a God-given talent.'

The wise man turned to the king and said once again: 'My lord, genius is made, not born. It is through forming a new habit, through repetition and practice, that I have conditioned myself.'

ILLUSION SEVEN: THE WEED FIGHTS THE FAT

When you stop smoking friends look serious and may warn you that you'll pile on the pounds. Come on, now, there is absolutely no reason why you should gain weight when you stop smoking. True, some people do, but that is only because they use the wrong method. The wrong methods can leave you feeling deprived and uncomfortable, and in these circumstances it's quite natural and fairly common to look around for something to ease the discomfort. Hence comfort food, the nibbles and bigger meals that are often used as a replacement. However, when you change the way you think and feel about smoking, you will not need the emotional comfort of eating as a substitute for smoking. I lost four stone *and* stopped smoking. These two things happened because I didn't have the wish to smoke any longer and I had no desire to replace the smoking with another equally bad habit. The Jeremiahs who predict that you're in for obesity if you stop should look at the health and weight studies. These show that weight loss among smokers in the long term is less sustainable than among non-smokers.

CHAPTER 19

Putting it together

May I repeat that the two roots to the smoking habit are the psychological and the physical. Up to this point you have been considering your mind. You have been dealing with the psychological root, and although I'll continue to help you with that part, let's get on now with the physical root. It's not that one is more important than the other. They are a dangerous double act!

CHANGING BRANDS

From now on, whenever you buy a packet of cigarettes, go to a shop that you have never visited before, even if this means a detour, a short drive or a bus ride. When you get there, instead of buying your usual brand, select a different brand, just any brand. And every time you buy a new packet, pick a different brand.

CALCULATING YOUR INHALATIONS

For the next 24 hours write down the number of inhalations you take from every cigarette.

For example:

Inhalations taken from every cigarette 10, 9, 10, 9, 8, 11, 10, 9, 8, 10,

Inhalations taken from every cigarette? _____

YOUR DATE WITH DESTINY

Take the highest number of inhalations. You are going to use this number as the number of days before you stop smoking for good.

For example:

Highest number from the example above is 11, which would mean in 11 days from now you would stop smoking.

Numbers of days before you stop smoking? _____

REDUCING THE NICOTINE DRUG

Take the number of cigarettes you smoke per day from your 48-hour cigarette calculation. In our example it was 22.

Average number of cigarettes _____

This is the maximum number of cigarettes you can smoke per day and every day until you stop smoking.

Take the highest number of inhalations from your 24-hour inhalation calculation. In our example it was 11.

Highest number of inhalations _____

This is the highest number of inhalations that you can take from every cigarette you smoke for the rest of today. Tomorrow reduce by one inhalation every cigarette you smoke, smoking no more than your average number. The next day reduce by another one inhalation, smoking no more than your average number of cigarettes. So if you start your first day on 9 inhalations per cigarette, on day two you smoke 8 inhalations every cigarette and day 3 no more than 7 inhalations every cigarette. Continue to do this until you no longer smoke and you have reached your date with destiny.

ASSUME THE POSITION

From now on each and every time you have a cigarette, you need to assume the stopping smoking position.

1. Do not talk or communicate with anyone while you are smoking or even holding a cigarette.

2. Do not watch television, use the computer or drive while smoking.

3. No smoking in your house, only smoke outside, and vary the place you smoke as much as possible.

4. If you do not smoke in the house and smoke only outside, stand 2ft away from the wall and face the wall while smoking.

Reducing your smoking intake by one puff per day will gradually lower your nicotine addiction levels, shrinking the smoking devil day by day until he becomes so small that he's not even noticeable.

NO SHARING

Between now and stopping smoking do not offer or accept cigarettes from anyone. Very soon you will no longer smoke and will not have any cigarettes to offer. And I want the people with whom you socialise to get used to the fact that you are stopping, so if anyone offers you a cigarette simply say: 'No thanks, I'm stopping soon.'

REMINDER JAR

Find an empty jar, an old jam jar or something similar with a screw-top lid. Half-fill this with water and 24 hours before you stop smoking use it as your ashtray. When you stop smoking have a good sniff of the jar every morning and evening. Thus you use the disgusting smell to remind you of what you have left behind.

This is a simple and easy programme to follow. It's worth the effort. As you follow all the guidelines you will become more aware of your smoking than ever before. The habit will be in sharp focus because you will be transferring it from your unconscious to your conscious. You will lower the physical addiction gradually so that your body can stop without any withdrawal. You will have weaned the nicotine out of your system.

Then as you switch the psychological from your unconscious to your conscious you can then take the things you don't want on the inside and put them on the outside. And you can lift the things you see on the outside and store them on the inside so that you stop smoking for ever.

CREATIVE VISUALISATION

1. Picture in your mind a cigarette, just one single cigarette. Imagine it on a table that's right in front of you.

2. When you can see, sense or imagine the cigarette on the table in front of you, focus on it more and more intently so that you're concentrating on the cigarette to the exclusion of everything else.

3. Now imagine the cigarette starting to roll away from you, slowly at first.

4. Watch as the cigarette rolls further and further away from you towards the edge of the table.

5. As you concentrate ever more deeply, notice the cigarette moving as if it is being pulled by an imaginary force.

6. This cigarette represents all the cigarettes in the world to you, and you can choose when you are ready to let it topple off the table.

7. Just pretend that once this cigarette falls off the table, all the cigarettes in the world will soon no longer exist for you.

Repeat this visualisation daily for the next month

STAYING STOPPED

CHAPTER 20

Never again

Now that your thinking has changed you will glance back at your smoking days and see them as a negative part of your life. You will see the present as having the benefit of not smoking. In fact, the 'not' part of your new life is the positive part as it enables you to feel better, do more things and achieve more goals. As I said before, you haven't given up something. You've thrown something into the bin and made important gains. It's worth keeping, guarding and nurturing those acquisitions and staying stopped.

When I stopped smoking I made a promise to myself. Breathing better, walking better and feeling happier, I decided I would never have even one cigarette again. I would never inhale a cigarette even once more. The logic is quite simple. If I never had one cigarette again I knew I could never become a smoker again. That's an absolute truth.

Do you fancy trying smoking again? Let me put it another way. How many times would you want to put your hand on a red hot oven ring to prove to yourself that you must not touch it? You would do that only if you were out of your mind. The hot ring would burn you and cause such an injury that you might lose your hand. What's the difference? Take the first cigarette and it will lead to more. The eventual injury could be bronchitis, emphysema or lung cancer. Your lung might have to be cut out and you might lose your life.

No, you wouldn't want to endure that, so I'll assume you won't want to start again. However, the smoking phenomenon is all around you and you have a good friend who has also stopped smoking. He has made a wise decision too, but one fine day he is tempted to have another cigarette. What advice would you give him? Or you have another good friend, a non-smoker, who is thinking about starting. What is the advice you would you give him?

CHAPTER 21
Inoculate yourself

When you inoculate a patient against a bug you treat the body with a vaccine to produce immunity. I don't know what particular challenges you have encountered previously, I don't know their context and I don't know what the content of the challenges were that you may have found difficult to overcome.

Maybe you have not had any challenges and you haven't given it any thought, or maybe you have. As I said, I don't know, but I do know that the vaccine is to have a solution beforehand, an effective way to ensure you don't catch the disease of smoking and start smoking again. It is so true that to be forewarned is to be forearmed.

Let us look at some scenarios and how you might handle them.

Other smokers, with all their influences and treacherous ways, are part of your life. Often they want to be in your scene because nobody likes being left behind. They feel as if you're having a party and they haven't been invited. They see that you have stopped smoking and perhaps they have failed in their attempts, but they certainly won't admit it. They may offer you a cigarette, and that's at best thoughtless and at worst cruel. They may say: 'Just have one.' That type will say anything to start you off again. I always found the best way to deal with this was to say: 'It's easy to stop smoking. Let me tell you how I did it.'

Here's another strategy that I found really helpful. Every time I saw a smoker with a cigarette in his mouth I pictured it as a rolled-up £50 note being burnt. I reasoned that the one cigarette represented £50 or more because it would lead to the next and ultimately many more. I'll ask you to be daring for a moment. Take a £50 note, roll it up like a cigarette and set fire to it. I'll bet you wouldn't do it. But why not try this experiment? You certainly do this if you are a smoker. Once I had used this tool it didn't bother or tempt me in the slightest when I saw other people smoking. I would smile to myself as I watched the £50 note between their lips smouldering away and being reduced to a pile of ash. No, I wasn't gloating, just being realistic – and grateful.

Situations in which alcohol is drunk could be dodgy. Maybe you had created an association between smoking and drinking and used to find it hard to not smoke when you have a drink. So what could you do to ensure that you were never tempted to have even one cigarette? That was Paula's problem. She said her biggest challenge was going out with her friends on Friday and Saturday nights. They would go on a pub crawl and she found smoking was then inevitable.

On the next page make a list of scenarios that are potentially a challenge or have been a challenge in the past, such as drinking in a bar or having a meal.

INOCULATION

CHAPTER 22
Staying a winner

The words you use are important. We have already said that words are symbols, and although they are just that, what they represent is important. When, therefore, you declare you're giving up something you're sending a signal to your mind saying: 'I'm missing out on something, I'm being deprived, I have to give it up.' But remember the natural reaction to this decision. When we feel deprived or think we are going to lose something we fight harder to hold on to it. Most of us would try harder to hold on to £1,000 than to earn £1,000.

That feeling of deprivation is a powerful one. If you feel deprived you want the object you are discarding even more. When I lost four stone and trained my body so that I could become a competitive body-builder, I would compete in different weight categories. I had to make the correct weight in order to compete, and this process took a great deal of discipline, hard work and determination. During the 16 weeks that I took to prepare myself for a competition, I followed a meticulously planned and organised nutritional eating regime. Obviously, it meant no chocolate, crisps, cakes or anything that would impede my weight loss. However, although I would eat those things only when I knew I could not have them, I felt deprived and as soon as I felt deprived I wanted them more. That's how it works when you say you're giving up something. The thoughts are actually negative. The solution involves a change in perception. That thinking is echoed throughout this book. I learnt to associate pleasure with reaching my competition weight and pain with eating the foods that had to be excluded.

There is a very definite way of saying this. You're not giving up a positive, you're choosing to leave behind a negative. Now think of your smoking. You're not giving up smoking because there is nothing valuable to give up. Nor are you losing anything. Regard your stopping as gaining. You are gaining better health, more wealth and a greater feeling of well-being. Have you booted out that feeling of deprivation? There is literally nothing to lose now. You are only reconditioning your thoughts to resemble those you had before you started smoking.

You may not be a veteran but you have all the knowledge and equipment because you have just used it to quit the habit yourself. You can tell your friends about altered attitudes to smoking, which can change even the habits and patterns stored in the unconscious part of the mind, and you can inform them of the benefits that are so valuable that cigarettes should never get in their way. You can tell them they have been taken in by illusions about smoking, seven illusions that you know of. Do your friends a favour and buy them this book as a gift, and it will make you feel even better.

WARNING!!
You have stopped smoking. Read the rest of the book only if you want to achieve more powerful, positive and permanent changes in other areas of your life.

CHANGE YOUR LIFE FOR GOOD

CHAPTER 23

Now you have a springboard

Most smokers consider stopping smoking as one of the greatest achievements in their lives.

You have already made significant positive changes in the way you think, act and behave in your life. You may want to continue to make other positive changes and achieve more or just enjoy life where you are at. The choice is yours.

So what next, where do you go from here? Well, wherever you want to go, it's entirely up to you.

First, just take a look at where you are now. You've stopped smoking and you can be pleased with yourself. One might even say you can be ecstatic about beating the habit that's been a millstone clinging around your neck for so long. Without that millstone you can do whatever you like, whether this means merely carrying on doing the things you enjoy or setting yourself another goal.

You don't need to feel obliged to climb to great heights, but do be aware that you can use stopping smoking as a springboard to achieving other successes in life. If there are other ambitions you are aching to achieve, then why not? Take stock for a moment. There was a time when maybe you thought you could not stop smoking, but you've actually done it. So now you can quite happily think of the many other things in your life that you want to change, stop doing or even start doing. Yet before you quit smoking you thought they were out of your reach.

The chaos theory in mathematics tells us there is a principle called the butterfly effect. The principle is that a small flap of a butterfly's wings on one side of the world causes a chain of events leading to a large-scale phenomenon, maybe a tornado, thousands of miles away on the other side. The conclusion is that, had the butterfly not flapped its wings, the trajectory of the wind might have been vastly different. It's an ominous thought.

You can experience something similar in your life. If you wish, you can use stopping smoking as a springboard to jump right into making other fantastic positive changes. After all, the basic change that you made was in what you believe. You once believed that you could not stop smoking and now you have. So what else do you want that you do not believe you can achieve? Apply another analogy. Imagine your achievement of stopping smoking as a snowball perched on the top of a high snow-covered mountain. You give the snowball a nudge and it starts to roll down the mountain. The snowball begins its journey slowly but soon gathers pace, and on the way it gathers more snow. In a short time, as the roll speeds up into a rush, the helter-skelter snowball becomes a boulder. Eventually, the snowball races down the mountain, growing in size and strength and sweeping away everything before it. You may think that's dramatic, it is. Stopping smoking is dramatic, so why not continue with dramatic thoughts? It's not too fanciful to imagine stopping smoking as the snowball that can become your avalanche to achieve anything you want in life.

Bright ideas

Before you move on to achieving another goal, do something quite uncomplicated at home. Just cast your eyes around you. You probably do this every day without any sense of wonder. This time look carefully at the room where you're sitting. Take in the wall coverings, the bricks, the furnishings, your clothes. Does every-thing look a little different now? Unless you live naked in a bare cave, these are all man-made things. Think a little more about them. If they are man-made, somebody, somewhere, had a bright idea. Then that individual, or others, took the idea and developed it into a reality. Perhaps that will give you the sense of wonder.

Perhaps, too, you're thinking a touch more about the world around you. Are your thoughts zooming back in time? Travel as far as the dawn of civilisation as we know it and you'll find an imaginative individual who had a hell of an idea. The wheel! If he or she had done nothing, our world today would be a totally different place. Everywhere you look there are wheels – bikes, buses, shopping trolleys, aeroplanes, wheelbarrows. A little while after that invention another individual would have had the idea of a rotating axle smeared with animal fat to reduce friction. The snowball had started to roll. Just for your amusement may I mention another of life's great innovations and add a lighter touch. What did the person who first had the idea of milking a cow think he was doing? A bizarre practice or innocent curiosity? I leave that to your vivid imagination! Whatever it was, we must feel grateful every time we drink tea or eat a pudding!

There is, however, a problem with ideas. Don't be blasé or careless about them, because they are fragile and sensitive little things. Like the first shoots from a seedling they are easily trampled on and killed. You have to look after them. So how do you protect them? Perhaps it is a good time to quote Zig Ziglar, the veteran American author and motivational speaker: 'It's not what happens to you that determines how far you will go in life. It is how you handle what happens to you.'

Bear Ziglar in mind when that flash of inspiration strikes you. With those words buzzing in your ears, you'll appreciate that the first and most important step is to capture your ideas. Think of the puffball seeds of a dandelion. When they first appear they are relatively stable and can be harvested a head at a time, but you know how delicate they are. Leave them a day or two and the first gentle breeze will carry them off to all the corners of your garden and you won't be able to collect them. You lose them if you hesitate. So it is with ideas. You don't want to lose them like the dandelion seeds.

The procedure for harvesting ideas is dead easy. You just write them down as key words no matter where you are and the instant that they occur. Imagine. While you are sitting on a train or sipping coffee in a bar you suddenly jump up and have to put your idea in writing. Perhaps you fear you'll look silly performing those antics but the lively-minded individual who first thought of the personal stereo or discovered how to make plastic didn't worry. Why should you? Temporary embarrassment means nothing.

The must is to carry a small notebook and pen wherever you go. They are essentials to all ideas people. Keep them beside your bed and even in the bathroom. Write down just enough to remind you of the idea later. Again, don't worry about embarrassment if anybody reads your scribbles. As soon as you can, transfer these key words into a proper notebook and expand on them. The discipline is vital – it could make you a multi-millionaire. Avoid the temptation to edit as you go, because self-critical editing has aborted many good ideas. You need to have the raw idea in front of you.

Ignore no new ideas, even though some will drag you into a dead end. If the notion that came to you in the middle of the night is doomed to lose its lustre by the harsh light of day, jot it down anyway. Maybe the time and circumstances are not appropriate for it at the moment. It may truly be an idea ahead of its time. No matter, make a record of it.

The next and equally important stage of what I call the RSPI – the Royal Society for the Protection of Ideas – is to conduct a regular review of what you have written. You'll be amazed at how often two seemingly unrelated ideas, several weeks or months apart, can suddenly blend to produce a third that is greater than the original sum of the two parts.

Now for the next big step. It may spur you on if you think of ideas in this way. No matter how great or small your ideas may be, they will achieve nothing except profits for the paper and ink manufacturers if all you do is write them down. Think action and get weaving! No matter how hesitant that first action step may be, just take it. It is only then that you can begin to see the true potential of an idea. Share it in confidence with a trusted friend or three, but choose your confidants with care. The world is full of other people's great ideas, thanks to a minority of unscrupulous thieves and plagiarists.

The time may not be right. So, if necessary, put your idea back in the incubator for a while and try again later.

Of course there will be all sorts of hurdles to jump. Think back to Edmund Hillary. Everest was one of the planet's biggest challenges but he refused to take no for an answer and he got to the top. Among your barriers will be the pooh-pooh people. Beware the 'friends' who delight in raining on your parade. Some will pour scorn on your idea because they hadn't thought of it first, so perhaps you should question their friendship. I once heard that Adam was created first, because the last thing that was needed in the Garden of Eden was a second opinion! The ridicule of others goes into the same waste bin as the embarrassment you may have felt when you leapt up in a crowded train to commit your ideas to paper. If you have faith in your concept just ignore the people who laugh at you. Be objective. Ridicule is negative, but suggestions, even if not well meant, should be evaluated.

In fact, invite friends to give you their ideas. What are real friends for? Your own original slant may change their non-starter into a fantastic breakthrough that will benefit mankind and make you wealthy beyond your wildest dreams. So give serious thought to even the most way-out thoughts.

Ideas, however, must not be remote things left sitting on the shelf or languishing in a drawer. That's no way to treat a potential world-beater. Ideas need light, air and a regular feed of creative thought. Here is an example of an idea that, sooner or later, will surely become reality. When it does, remember that you read it here first!

It all started recently when I read a report that more than 4,000 bank branches in Britain had been closed between 1997 and 2007. A month later I learnt from a radio news item that the shutters had been brought down on a similar number of sub-post offices. Most of us have had the experience of seeing a bank branch or post office shut down. How we cursed the decision. If you live in a village that has lost its bank you may be forced to travel five miles or more to your nearest branch. And what about the arthritic old ladies who depend on their neighbourhood post office for stamps and envelopes? Some even need their post offices for their old age pensions if they don't have bank accounts. When I heard the news about the closures my key words, in embryonic scribble, read: 'Banks and POs, similar products, money/services.'

I thought even better of my idea when I saw that one of the official bodies responsible for rural affairs was predicting the demise of 20 per cent of all village stores within a few years. That was the real stimulus to get me going. It's odd how bad news can shake you into thinking constructively.

Here's the idea that evolved and blossomed. The government and a consortium of banks or the National Lottery or both should fund couples to operate an empty village store as a money shop. Every shop owner-manager would receive a salary and would be exempt from business rates. Every shop would provide the top ten main banking services and the top ten post office services. Any profits would be shared equally between the government and the owner-manager. Is that really so far-fetched? At first sight the government would probably tear it up and forget it, or am I being cynical?

However, just ponder on the advantages to the nation and the individual. A chain of these money shops would stem the decay of village life, provide a service that has been denied tens of thousands, maybe millions, of people, and challenge monopolistic organisations. I have to admit, of course, that a project of this size and importance could not go on the road without serious research. The first action step, therefore, would be to gain more hard information and facts. If the proposal was shown to be economically sensible the next move would be to organise a group of individuals with the necessary skills and experience to form a lobby group. These people would need to be gutsy and determined as well as clued-up and would have to be certain that the proposal would work. The rest of it you can only imagine. And it would all be because of a brainwave idea, turning into a huge boon to society.

The idea may have sounded far-fetched a moment ago. Do you still think it's crazy? Tell Peter Wood, who came up with the Direct Line insurance concept and then sold to Royal Bank of Scotland for millions, that he was crazy. Suppose you had said that to Freddie Laker, who was the innovator in cut-price scheduled air travel. Tell it to the co-founders of Google.com, who took the concept of an internet search engine to hitherto unscaled heights. Tell it to the founders of Freeview digital television. Tell it to Jacqui Gold, who built the Ann Summers chain to sell erotic goods to women, when this kind of market had previously been exclusive to dodgy males in belted raincoats in dark Soho shops. Get the point? All these big money-spinners came from ideas that probably flashed into the heads of Laker and the others at the most unlikely times and in the most unlikely places. The chances are, too, that these lively spirits noted down their smart ideas as they thought of them. Is my idea sounding more attractive now?

The very originality of an idea often shoos it out of court for some people. That's a mistake. Don't let even the outlandishness of an idea put you off. The fact that something hasn't been done before doesn't mean it cannot or should not be done. Even if it is already being done, look for an innovative twist. Do it bigger or smaller, brighter or dimmer. If it's electric, try clockwork. Remember what Trevor Bayliss did with his radio. Thanks to Bayliss you can now take a radio into the poorest parts of Africa without depending on an electricity supply or batteries. If something is manual, try making it electric, just like the guy who motorised shredders.

As you can see, every action or every dream begins as an idea. If the original thinkers had told themselves the idea was impossible where would we be today? We could be rubbing along without cars, trains, television, bottles of milk, calculators and even the wheel. You thought you couldn't stop smoking, but you did it. That was an achievement, wasn't it? Clap yourself on the back if you like. Then if you have other cherished goals, remember how you kicked the weed and use the same determination to reach them.

The next essential is a good plan. When we decided to enlarge our house the logical choice was to extend, so we hired an architect. The architect sat down with my wife and I and began by asking us questions. What was the purpose of the extension? Why did we want what we would use it for? He went into all the specifics. He covered the total size, the layout and the dimensions of every room. He included the smallest of details, such as where the electricity sockets should be. He wrote down every detail so that he could produce his grand plan with confidence. He looked at the resources we had and how much we could invest. He considered how best to utilise the existing property. He seized on any opportunities that could be included so as to maximise the possibilities. He took away all these details to begin drafting a blueprint to place before us. When he came back we discussed any changes and he tweaked the blueprint a little.

Once we had approved the blueprint the plans were submitted and we hired a quantity surveyor to calculate the costs with a view to getting best value for money. The quantity surveyor worked with a colleague and they calculated what materials were required down to the very last brick and the length of time it would take to complete the project. That was superb precision work.

The moral? When the idea takes on some flesh and bones, plan with great care and caution how you will bring it to fruition. When you build an extension, whether it's to your house, mind or life, you begin with a concept, which is the blueprint of what it is to become. Without a concept you cannot know what the end result will look like, or whether it will fulfil your purpose. The blueprint is the first step in laying the foundation.

It's your dream

Pretty well all of us have goals and ambitions, of course. In fact, you'd be mighty unenterprising if you didn't have something to go for. I don't know how many goals you have or what your goals are, but let us say one of your ambitions is to be super-rich. I'm sure that strikes a chord with most of you.

A great model for anybody wishing to acquire heaps of wealth is John Robert Madejski, a man who likes to call himself a successful businessman rather than an entrepreneur. He was born in Stoke-on-Trent, in the British Midlands, in 1941. The blinding flash struck him while he was on holiday in Florida in the mid-1970s. He saw a car sales magazine that included pictures of the vehicles for sale. To many people that format would mean nothing, but Madejski was an ideas man.

Madejski casually flicked through the magazine and suddenly the concept was there. He would produce a similar magazine for the UK. It was a simple idea but it was a great idea. He flew home and founded *Thames Valley Trader* in 1976. Madejski began by thinking big and used the magazine in its infancy to sell cars, houses and anything else that anyone wanted to bring into the marketplace. Even aircraft were advertised for sale in the magazine. A little later the magazine concentrated exclusively on vehicles, and it was renamed *Auto Trader*. In 1998 Madejski sold his publishing company for £174 million. He had a concept, worked at it with a single-minded enthusiasm and built huge wealth.

Madejski, now best known as the chairman of Reading football club, is named in the 2007 *Sunday Times Rich List* as one of the UK's 200 wealthiest people. His net worth is said to be in the region of £400 million. Madejski came up with an idea. The result of sticking with it and following it through is the multi-million-pound fortune. Worth it? If your aim is to be super-rich there is only one answer to that.

I don't know what you want, but whatever it is you have to make the moves. It's all too easy to blurt out the negatives. You can talk for ever about why you can't have it or get it or why it's out of your reach. You can drone on about why others can achieve it, but you say you're different. You grumble to yourself: 'I don't have fantastic educational qualifications, I don't have money to start, I don't have . . .'

Come on, that's just pointless griping. It gets you nowhere, which is hardly where you want to go if you have an ambition. I do know that you have the potential to achieve it. When *The Sunday Times Rich List* started, most of the people included in it had inherited their wealth. In the 2007 list about 75 per cent of the people are self-made multi-millionaires and billionaires. You complained you lack the academic qualifications, so were they all highly educated? Look at the evidence. Most of these self-made mega-rich people were under-achievers at school. They had that valuable something else that we've been talking about. They all had the concept that something had to change and, what was more, it was up to them. This involved setting themselves a goal. To achieve it they took the necessary action, which often meant working hard for that goal. So can you.

Take your cue, if you prefer, from the great Walt Disney. He said: 'If you can dream it, you can do it.' Without doubt, that's a good place to start. It may help to say Disney's words over and over again.

You should, however, ask yourself something else to be certain you're doing the right thing. Does your goal inspire you? Do you feel delighted and excited at the prospect of achieving it? If so, then it's an important goal, one that's worth reaching for. Maybe you say to yourself: 'It would be nice but I'm not really bothered one way or the other.' If you do, the goal is not a goal at all.

The apathetic individual won't get there. How can you get there if you don't know where you want to go? That's basic common sense, isn't it? To accomplish what you set out to do you must have a clearly defined result in view. May I hark back to Edmund Hillary again? Goals can seem like mountains to climb, but with consistent action it becomes easier to reach the summit. The mountains have not become smaller. Instead, you have grown to conquer them, and with growth you expand your skills.

One thing to remember always is that the right attitudes hit the target. This came home to me vividly when I was invited to talk to a group of successful businessmen about the power of the mind. The best part of these occasions is often the coffee break when individuals can speak to you without inhibition. It was while we were among the coffee cups that one of the delegates approached me and began talking. I knew this man was a high achiever, a multi-million-pound serial entrepreneur. He had started with nothing but now had a net worth of more than £10 million.

As we chatted he told me something that I didn't know about him. Less than five years earlier he had lost everything he had made. What followed was intriguing. This amazing man told me what he had learnt from the experience. He had come back from losing his fortune when most people would have crawled away to hide under a stone and lick their wounds. Not him. 'What on earth did you do?' I asked. He looked at me for a moment as he puzzled over my question almost as if it was out of place. Then he replied calmly: 'The most important lesson I learnt was not accumulating all that wealth. The most important lesson I learnt was to have a millionaire mindset.' Now that's the attitude that says it all.

You can squeeze out the very juice of life when your goal meets the following criteria, which are the core ingredients in a blueprint. Led Zeppelin sang *Stairway to Heaven*, and perhaps now it will mean something to you. With that mindset you can consistently and successfully achieve anything you want.

CHAPTER 24

Achieving the goals

- What: This must be specifically stated in the positive.
- When: You must allot a period of time for your achievement.
- Who: The effort must be self-initiated and maintained and controlled by you.
- Why: The reasons or purpose or benefits must be clearly set out.
- How: Action is necessary, your goals have to be realistic and attainable, you need to call up all your resources and you must be flexible.
- Assessment: How will your life be affected if you achieve your goals – or don't achieve them?

Now for details

It's time to be more precise. Perhaps it goes without saying, but when you define something you state clearly what it is. If I asked you what you want it's no good saying: 'Everything.' You have to define your aims or ambitions or desires specifically.

So think about what you want in three areas of your life:

- **Career:** Decide the path you want to take in your occupation or job and treat it as a long-term activity.
- **Lifestyle:** Split your time between your working life and your enjoyment of the things you have achieved – the toys, the house, the cars, electronic equipment, holidays.
- **Personal life:** Think of your health and your relationships with your partner, friends and family.

When you are making your decisions remember that the only real barriers are the limitations you place on yourself. The can-do process can now get under way. If the goal is specific it starts to become tangible. Put it all into words, describing what you hope to see, hear and feel. When you have incorporated all the detail you will have made a transformation. You will have taken the invisible and turned it into the visible. You will have broken out of the straitjacket.

Be the architect of your destiny

A little story may help you to see the importance of having specific objectives. A young man called Ryan came to see me saying he was lost. This lost soul said he didn't know what to do. That's a telltale sign if ever there was one. Like many others he found that what he was actually doing was nothing! Not the best way to achieve anything. Here is how our conversation went.

Elliott	'So what is it you really want, Ryan?'
Ryan	'I want more money.'
Elliott	'Why do you want more money?'
Ryan	'So that I can have a better life.'
Elliott	'What would a better life look like to you?'
Ryan	'I'd have money to do more things.'
Elliott	'So if you had more money what would you do that you don't do now?'
Ryan	'I would live in a nicer house.'
Elliott	'Anything else?'
Ryan	'I would drive a new car.'
Elliott	'Anything else?'
Ryan	'I would spend more time with my wife and family.'
Elliott	'Anything else?'
Ryan	'I would take my family on holiday.'
Elliott	'Anything else?'
Ryan	'Well, that's quite a lot, isn't it?'
Elliott	'OK, so let's just focus on these for a moment.'

Ryan's replies were really quite revealing. Look carefully at the transcript above. We started with Ryan's goal of wanting more money. With persistent questions we began to chunk down. When you chunk down you get a flavour of the solution. You may love pineapples, but you couldn't get a whole one into your mouth in one go. Therefore, you reduce it to chunks and then you can eat it and taste it. By chunking down Ryan's global goal of wanting more money, we began to make it specific to him, lasering his scope and fixing his sights on the specifics that made up his goal. Clearly, when Ryan said bluntly that he wanted more money his answer was too generalised to ignite him. How much more money was enough? Even if he had said he wanted lots more his approach would still have been too vague and general. But when I asked him what he would do with more money we started chipping away at the purpose for the extra shekels.

Poor Ryan, I kept at him. I wanted to know why more money would give him a better life. How much more money would he require? What would that better life consist of? If he knew that, would he want double his present earnings? Treble his earnings? Maybe ten times? He needed to be more definite about that good life.

What about that new car that Ryan wanted to drive? The conversation continued.

Elliott	'Would any car do? Would you drive one of those old-fashioned three-wheelers, or a Skoda perhaps? Or would you prefer a Mini or a Range Rover? Which new car specifically do you want?'
Ryan	'A Mercedes.'
Elliott	'Which Mercedes?'
Ryan	'A Mercedes 500SL.'
Elliott	'Nice choice. What colour?'
Ryan	'Blue.'
Elliott	What colour would the interior be?'
Ryan	'Black leather.'
Elliott	'How much are these cars?'
Ryan	'About £70,000.'
Elliott	'And how much more money do you need if you're going to spend that much on a car?'

We went on and on until we had acquired all the information needed. I'm sure Ryan finished up appreciating that I had needed to draw out the specifics. I tried to make his vision as rich, vivid and colourful as possible. I wanted him to reach out in his mind and touch the car, smell the leather interior, feel the steering wheel in his hands. I wanted him to imagine driving along with the top down in the fresh summer breeze. The individual with an ambition needs to know what it will be like when he has reached his goal, what it will look like and feel like. Ryan, with his ambition to have more money, needed to know what difference the achievement would make to his life and the lives of those for whom he cared.

When Ryan left me after this benevolent interrogation he still had his dream but he had a pretty clear idea of what the dream was made of. He was better equipped than when he walked in. When you make your goal specific you have a greater chance of accomplishment. He understood that too. If you're using a sporting analogy, you could say that without a goal you're not playing football – you're just kicking a ball around the park.

Time is of the essence

All right, you know everything about your goal, and you're going for it. But how will you know when you get there? And how will you know the length of time it will take?

Those are reasonable concerns, but if you have an overall plan you will find your answers. The first thing to be sure of is that your goals are measured. The method you choose for measuring will depend on the actual goal and could include one or more of the following – quantity, time, intensity and productivity. If you're serious about your goal you have to stay on track, so you need a yardstick. If you are still unsure whether your goal is measurable, you can ask yourself several questions. How much? How many? And then, how will I know when it is accomplished?

There's a good example from athletics. You wouldn't have a sprinter competing at the Olympics without a timekeeper. Imagine how the result would read. You would see that X came first, Y was second and H finished in third place. But that would be only half the story. You would want to know how quick these runners were so that you could compare their times against the times of other athletes over the same distance, perhaps even against your own speed and abilities.

Time for a recap. When you write down your goals and you get clear vision and focus, you are enabled to create an action plan. An important part of that plan is to break down your goal into easy manageable stages. You can prioritise the stages and as you pass every milestone you grow in confidence.

YOUR GOALS:
WHAT DO YOU WANT?

CAREER

LIFESTYLE

PERSONAL LIFE

CHAPTER 25

Down to you

Here is another of the realities you have to face if you are going for a target. You know you can change yourself but you cannot make somebody else change. The best you can hope for is that another individual who sees your personal change will be inspired to change too. Be reconciled to the prospect of being on your own. If you are going to reach your goal you must not be reliant on somebody else. The whole thing must be initiated by you and then maintained and controlled by you.

What is more, the striving for a goal and effecting any changes in your life must be carried out by you and for you. So is it you who wants to hit that target? This is vital, and it's not a case of being selfish. One reason is that if your goal is for somebody else it is unlikely that you will inject the necessary emotional intensity. Let's go back to where we came in – stopping smoking. A man says his goal is to quit. You probe a little and ask him why he should take such a step. He shifts a little uneasily from one foot to another and says his wife wants him to stop. Then you ask him: 'But do you want to stop?' He's uneasy again and finally admits: 'Not really.' Sadly then, the goal is not important enough to him. It's a meaningless goal. There are, of course, odd exceptions. The one certain thing is that it's up to you to be the judge and jury on whether the goal is for you or somebody else.

Why and how

That's established then. The goals are most successfully pursued if they are for you. Now ask yourself how important your goals are to you and what you would be willing to sacrifice to achieve them. I have to admit this is something of an acid test.

Would you be willing to sacrifice an evening out with friends? What about scrapping a holiday if it got in the way? Would you go without the approval of others around you if that was necessary? Would you put your goals above a friendship? Or your relationship? In the end your feelings and emotions make the judgments and decisions.

Before you think I'm being extreme, let me assure you that I am not suggesting you have to leave your partner, or cut loose from your friends. I am not saying you should never have a holiday and that you walk around in complete isolation, doing nothing except working 70 hours a week. All that would be extreme. I'll put things in proportion. What I am asking you to do is to take a good hard look at what you want and think about what it means to you. Then you should decide what you would be prepared to do to achieve your ambition. It's not so difficult or drastic when you think of it in that way.

Don't do anything rash. In fact, before you do anything ask yourself why these goals are important to you. Remember that decision to quit smoking. Then you looked at the benefits of being free from the weed and decided you wanted them.

Perhaps you should take a step back and start by rooting out what is holding you back. People who accomplish extraordinary things are just ordinary folk who have developed the mindset that allows them to turn obstacles into stepping stones on the way to their goals. That mindset is so important, as it was to the multi-millionaire who lost everything and then got it back again. Indeed, of all the obstacles in the way of your unlimited potential the most harmful and corrosive is self-limiting belief.

If you think you can, or if you think you can't, you will be absolutely right! The American author Richard Bach takes this notion a stage further. His cautionary words: 'When you argue for your limitations, then, sure enough, they are yours.' Your self-limiting beliefs are as familiar as the sequence that you use for dressing. They are as comforting as having a furry dog sleeping across your feet as you relax in front of the television. You get used to them. For the moment you are in love with them and they are holding you back in that limited 10 per cent comfort zone. They are part of what makes you an individual. But you can change them.

You could adopt the mindset of Benazir Bhutto, the former Pakistani leader. Note the determination in her statement: 'I had faith in myself. I had always felt that I could become Prime Minister if I wanted.' And, of course, she did exactly that.

I want to return briefly to the idea that you can be, do or have whatever you want. There is a little caveat here, of course. I don't want to sound unreasonable! You will clearly need to operate within the realms of possibility. For example, you could decide to qualify as a doctor and as a lawyer. Admittedly, you could, but it would be daft to expect to do both at the same time. Do as others have before. First one, then the other. Obviously, you have to be practical but don't let this be an excuse for inaction. Beware that you are not seeing obstacles that are only in your mind.

Obstacles are there to be torn down. Begin by fearlessly examining any beliefs that you hold about yourself because they can be like brick walls to your progress. The earliest and possibly most deeply rooted ones were planted in your childhood, when a well-meaning parent, teacher or contemporary said: 'Boy are you clumsy.' The next time you dropped something your belief was confirmed. Oh dear, what a butter-fingers you were. Then, because you believed you were clumsy, you started dropping more things. More confirmation. Perhaps you can still recall that face-reddening, stomach-churning, pants-wetting moment when you dropped and smashed your Great-aunt Minnie's priceless, though hideous, vase. The chances are that she didn't go ballistic over the loss of the vase. There was something far more serious. Your Great-uncle Mickey's ashes were scattered all over the carpet! Now it was indelibly branded on your mind that you were clumsy, and you soon stopped handling anything. Fear grabs an impressionable child with such a grip. You were falsely limited . . . until now.

Just imagine for a moment that you are not clumsy and you never were, even when you wrote off that vile vase. This means your self-beliefs are not really yours. I am prepared to bet good money that the vast majority of your self-limiting beliefs originated from comments made by other people. They made their criticisms impulsively, even hysterically. Except they probably didn't know you at all. They were just reacting in a shallow way to some trivial event for which they thought you were to blame.

Think the word 'can' from now on. Immediately kill off 'can't' and eliminate it from your mental and spoken vocabulary. Replace it with 'can'. That sounds simple but it's a pivotal act representing a big change. The reason is that as soon as you remove your favourite self-limiting beliefs, you are also removing all your treasured excuses for not doing things.

At this point you should rewind to the beliefs and reasons section on how to stop smoking. You did that, didn't you? You can now use the same technique to aim for your new goal.

What are your reasons, the legs that support your beliefs?

REASONS FOR ACHIEVING YOUR GOAL

SCALE OF IMPORTANCE

Once you have covered the questions above, draw up a scale of one to ten. Ten means: 'It's really important to me and I will do whatever it takes ethically and responsibly to achieve it.' One means: 'It's not worth sacrificing anything to attain this goal.' Which number does each of your goals represent?

FOR EACH OF YOUR GOALS
ASK YOURSELF THE FOLLOWING QUESTIONS:

What will happen if you do?

What will happen if you don't?

What won't happen if you do?

What won't happen if you don't?

The way forward

You're on your way, you know where you want to get to, but how are you going to get there? Do you have a route map? What would have to happen if you're going to reach this particular goal?

I want to look at the way people reach their destinations. The psychologist and consultant Edward de Bono has something to say about this: 'The path from A to B is not the same as the paths from B to A. Imagine we have a tree that splits into branches, each of which splits into many twigs and then leaves. Imagine we have an ant sitting on the trunk of a tree. What are the chances of that ant reaching one specified leaf? At every branch junction the chances will diminish by one over the number of branches. Given an average tree, the chances are about one in 80,000 of reaching a particular leaf. But if we have the ant sitting on the leaf, what are the chances of that ant reaching the trunk of the tree? One in one!'

The ant would have to plan in monumental detail to arrive on that particular leaf. Not all planning has to be so complicated, but the principle remains that failing to plan is planning to fail.

The ant's journey is an extreme case meant to illustrate the point. Here's an example that will be much more familiar to most people. If you wanted to arrive at a particular street you might use an A–Z, or by courtesy of 21st-century technology you might have a satellite navigation system. Either way you would be using a map, and with your paper version or the satnav you would calculate the shortest or quickest route possible.

Perhaps you would be without a vehicle and your journey would involve a variety of transport methods. You could need buses or trains, so you would have to know the timetables and where the different modes of transport would take you. If you are on your own four wheels there could be roundabouts, junctions, bridges or other challenges along the way.

Right now you could be raising an eyebrow and recalling that every meticulously planned journey in the past has hit a hitch. Suppose a railway station is unexpectedly out of action. Floods and acts of terrorism have managed to sabotage your travel plans before now. Maybe a vital road on the route may be closed because a boozed motorist has caused carnage. What would you do? Would you give up? Or would you find a way around it? You might take a detour and then get yourself back on track. Faced with these little emergencies you would constantly check to see whether you were on course or to make sure of being on time for your next connection. In short, you would have a route map to get you there. Now apply the same model to your goal.

Fortune may be on your side. You can't count on it but Colin Powell, the former American Secretary of State, may have been right when he said: 'Luck tends to come to people that are well prepared.'

We've talked before about reducing a task to manageable chunks. And it's true that you can do anything if you break your goal into small enough chunks. So our next job is to create a route map or a blueprint of what you need to do to get from where you are to where you want to be. For the moment we won't bother with when it needs to be done – we'll come to that a little later. The first part of the operation is to write down in as much detail as possible everything that has to happen to carry you to your destination.

ROUTE MAP:
WHAT DO I NEED TO DO TO GET FROM WHERE I AM
TO WHERE I WANT TO BE?

The other way

'Here is Edward Bear coming downstairs behind Christopher Robin, bump, bump, bump on the back of his head. It is, as far as he knows, the only way of coming downstairs, but sometimes he feels there really is another way, if only he could stop bumping for a moment and think of it.' Do you recognise that delightful story from your childhood days? I couldn't resist quoting A.A. Milne's *Winnie-the-Pooh* because it says something about how you reach your goal.

As we found, problems often beset even a properly planned route. However, instead of surrendering at the first sign of trouble, it is constructive to regard a problem as just another opportunity to do something differently. A tweak here and a rethink there work wonders. When an aeroplane flies between two airports the flight path requires adjustment by the pilot 90 per cent of the time so that it arrives smoothly at the destination. Maybe the passengers shouldn't be told that, but they should be reassured to know that they touch down on terra firma safely thanks to the alertness of the pilot.

It is a fact of life that every solution has its problems. The problems make up the pattern of every achievement. Without daylight how can you appreciate darkness, without rain how can you appreciate sunshine? When there have been blocks and glitches in reaching a goal you cherish the accomplishment even more. When you make it to the other side and look back and see how far you have come, you feel the real joy. It's often said that you value highly something for which you have had to struggle. That's the principle. A problem is simply a challenge that you have to meet. It's the resolution that creates your revolution. As Richard Bach, who wrote *Illusions: The Adventures of a Reluctant Messiah*, says: 'Every problem in your life carries a gift inside.'

Consider your options. You could be tempted to think that there are only two options here. You either do it, or you do not. No, it's not as clear-cut as that.

This is your position now. You have defined your goals, the realities of the task and the resources you have. You are almost ready to start your journey towards achievement. First, however, you must attend to the flashing amber caution of available options, usually more than two of them! There is little point in applying energy, drive and direction to a difficult path if there is an easier route. Here are some examples of the type of questions that will help you to review your options:

Are there any other ways that I could set this goal?
Are there any other ways that I could achieve this outcome?
Have I listed all the alternatives, large or small, that might offer
    better solutions?
What else could I do if there were no time or cost constraints?
What could I do to remove or minimise these restraints?
What else could I do?
What else would I do?
Why have I chosen a particular alternative?

The whole point of the options checklist is to ensure that either you replace your original goal with a better one or you confirm to yourself that this goal really is achievable and worthwhile. We often say you should never take your eye off the ball when tackling a project. It's wise counsel. Always keep the end result or outcome in mind. At the same time, by growing in confidence as you pass every stage, you are also reinforcing your goal in your subconscious mind.

If you want something of a soundbite from an eminent source to highlight the importance of flexibility as you progress towards your goal, how about listening to Albert Einstein? The genius mathematician and physicist said: 'Our thinking creates problems that the same type of thinking will not solve.' I suppose that's what we mean today when we talk of thinking outside the box. It's exactly what you did when you stopped smoking.

Let me tell you another story. There was a small boy who banged a drum all day long and loved every moment of it. He would not stop the racket, no matter what the neighbours said or did. Anybody with a noisy child next door would appreciate how wearing that would be. Various people who called themselves Sufis – the genuine articles are Islamic mystics – and other well-wishers were called in by neighbours and asked to do something about the wretched rowdy child.

The first so-called Sufi told the boy that he would perforate his eardrums if he continued to make so much noise. This was a somewhat out-of-touch warning. The reasoning was too complex for the small child, who was neither a scientist nor a scholar!

The second told him that drum-beating was a sacred activity and should be carried out only on special occasions. Also rather out of touch with reality.

The third offered the neighbours plugs for their ears.

The fourth gave the boy a book.

The fifth gave the neighbours books that described a method of controlling anger through biofeedback.

The sixth gave the boy meditation exercises to make him placid and explained that all reality was imagination. Did he think this was likely to get through to the boy?

Every one of these suggested remedies worked for a while, but none of them lasted long. They certainly didn't help the neighbours, who just wanted the disturbance to stop.

Eventually, a real Sufi came along. He looked at the problem, handed the boy a hammer and chisel, and said: 'I wonder what is *inside* the drum.' What a wise man! With a little divergent thought he hit the target.

See how divergent you can be. Overleaf you will find nine dots. The challenge is to join all the nine dots together with four straight lines without taking the pen off the paper. Not easy. I have given you four copies so that you can try several times.

Outside the box

The French philosopher Etienne Souriau observed: 'Pour inventer il faut penser à côté.' To invent, you must think on the side. To us that means the route is not fixed, that it is necessary to have different perceptions, that you must not be boxed into conventional thinking. Souriau was right. Nothing new comes from sticking to old habits and practices.

You may need to change your thinking to eliminate the obstacles to your goal. We've already established that the route is not necessarily fixed and that the map is not the whole story. The ant can give us another illustration. When you tackle obstacles you can

go with the philosophy of this busy insect. Take a look at swarming ants on a path or in the garden some time and you may pick up a tip or two. When an ant has decided it wants to get somewhere it scurries in that specific direction. The ant, however, is too small to see a long way ahead and it always finds an obstacle in its way. This creature is not a quitter. When it comes up against a barrier it goes around one side or the other to stay on its route. It may go over or under or through the obstacle. If the obstacle is edible and digestible the resourceful ant will feed on it before it continues on its chosen path.

Your comfort zone may be your obstacle. There are two ways to look at this. The first is to step outside your comfort zone. Now, you may have tried that once or twice and decided you don't really want to be there. That's a natural enough reaction because, as the term indicates, you are not comfortable outside this zone. A better option is to expand your comfort zone gradually and progressively so that you can do more and step outside the original area.

Incidentally, here's a little diversion, the answer to the dots teaser – it involved moving out of the comfort zone and using a little imagination:

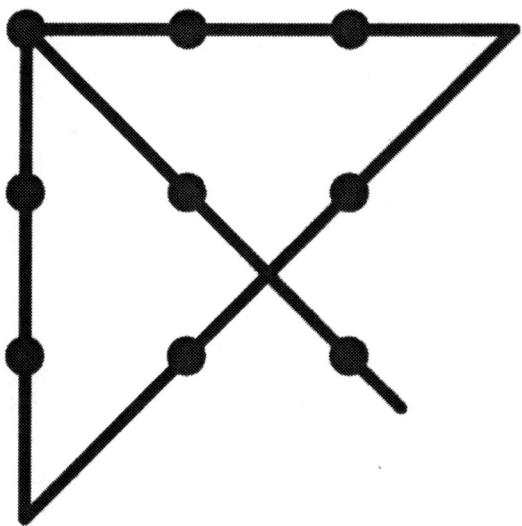

CHAPTER 26
No fear

We've looked at self-imposed limits before. Now I want to consider an emotion that is probably the biggest limit to achievement. It's the most common obstacle that people talk about on the inside. It's fear. Let's take a close look at this dangerous enemy and help you to break your box. Cut loose and you'll find you cannot hold on any longer to the position you previously occupied.

Fear was put into vivid perspective by the larger-than-life Second World War hero General George Patton. Old Blood and Guts, as he was known, said: 'Fear kills more people than death. Death kills us but once. And we usually don't even know it. But fear kills us over and over again, subtly at times and brutally at others. But if we keep trying to avoid our fears, they will chase us down like persistent dogs.'

I imagine everybody knows what the physical feeling of fear is like. Reading this, you are probably reliving your worst experience of it. Your stomach has butterflies, your breathing rate goes up, your heart pumps harder and faster. Maybe your hands start sweating. Maybe when you think about it you just can't sleep properly.

Take a step back now. What does the physical experience of excitement feel like? Your stomach has butterflies, your breathing rate goes up, your heart pumps harder and faster. Maybe your hands start sweating. Maybe when you think about it you just can't sleep properly. That's how you felt when you were waiting to go on a rollercoaster or ride a bike for the very first time. What have I just told you? You've got it – the two physical experiences are identical. Fear, therefore, is only a state of mind.

How you handle fear is up to you, but you can be in control. Fear can paralyse you, or you can choose to realise that the fear is a signal that you're about to break through. It may sound strange but you can actually welcome it. In our close look at fear I want to turn the microscope on the two most common versions that hold people back. They are the fear of failure and the fear of success.

No failure

Start by accepting that failure doesn't exist. In fact, if I were you I'd take drastic action. If you have a dictionary in your possession I recommend you take a thick black marker pen and strike through the word failure. Erase it from your life. Why do I say this? Let me tell you there is no such thing as failure, only feedback.

I know it's a bullish attitude but it's one you need if you're going to achieve anything worthwhile. Muhammad Ali, the former world heavyweight boxing champion, had something similar in mind when he said: 'There's nothing wrong with getting knocked down as long as you get right back up.'

Apply this bullishness to one of life's earliest struggles. Watch a young child learning to walk. You'll have done this if you're a parent. The child pulls himself up on a piece of furniture, takes a couple of steps and falls over. I'd be surprised if you shouted: 'Stop, you have failed at walking. Don't try it again.' Of course you don't. The child doesn't give up either. He pulls himself up again and takes another couple of steps. He falls over again. I'd be even more surprised if you shouted at him to stop at the second attempt too. I'm sure you wouldn't tell him: 'You have failed at walking again, so don't try any more.' No, you wouldn't. How many times do you let the child haul himself up? The answer is that you let the child try until he can put one foot in front of the other and stay upright. That's why we are able to walk. As I said, there is no such thing as failure.

When you're a passenger in a vehicle do you ever turn to the driver and ask how many times he took his driving test? What a cheek. It would be crass to ask the question. But if you happen to get a polite answer it would be even more crass to say: 'Oh no, I can't get into the car with you because it took you four attempts to pass your driving test.' Your attitude would not be merely crass. It would be very unenlightened. Did that man fail at driving? Certainly not, because through persistence he gained his licence. The following may have been his approach. If your first strategy does not reward you with your goal, replace it with a new strategy. If your new strategy is not successful, change it for another strategy, and so on. You should continue doing this until you find the one that works for you. Instead of giving cause for concern, your driver shows stickability and a steadiness that qualifies him to be on the road. He's a good example to others, and that's not meant to be patronising.

President John F. Kennedy is another good example. He had nagging and chronically painful back problems, but he was still able to do the most powerful and stressful job in the world. Olympic multi-gold-medallist Steve Redgrave is a diabetic, but he still achieved almost superhuman results.

An example of the success of tenacity is Thomas Edison, who created a world record of 1,093 patents for inventions, including the electric light bulb and the phonograph. He said: 'Genius is 1 per cent inspiration and 99 per cent perspiration.'

Edison hammered home the point when he was interviewed by a reporter. The journalist asked him: 'Mr Edison, do you feel like a failure and do you think you should just give up now?' Edison replied: 'Young man, why would I feel like a failure? And why would I ever give up? I now know definitively over 9,000 ways that an electric light bulb will not work. Success is almost in my grasp.' Shortly after that, and after more than 10,000 attempts, Edison invented the light bulb.

Sad Sanjay

Sanjay was sad when he came to see me. I understood the sadness as he told me he didn't have any confidence when it came to talking to women. Actually, it's more than sad. It's socially disabling for a healthy young man. He said: 'I just can't give women eye contact. I can't even look at them. I certainly can't approach a woman and I wouldn't know what to say. I'm just so afraid of being rejected.'

I had a plan for Sanjay. I asked him to play a game for the next two weeks before coming back to see me. I said to him: 'I want you to get yourself rejected by as many women as possible during the next two weeks. Talk to them, be polite, be nice, but I want you to try to get rejected. Your fear of being rejected can't arise because your goal is to get rejected and you'll be succeeding in that.' Sounds a little odd, doesn't it? Off he went all the same, determined to be rejected.

When Sanjay came back to see me I asked how he had got on, or, rather, not got on. He told me: 'I got rejected about ten times the first night I went out clubbing.'

'Great!' I said. 'Then what happened?' Sanjay went on: 'After a while it got easier. I even began to feel comfortable talking to the women I approached.'

'As you practised, you mean?' I asked. 'Yes,' replied Sanjay, 'and one woman gave me eye contact and I looked right back at her. Then I did it more and more, and by the second week I just couldn't stick to the goal of being rejected. There were times when I forgot and just carried on talking.' So no longer did Sanjay worry about being rejected by women.

The words of Sven-Göran Eriksson, the former England soccer boss, might have been intended for him: 'The greatest barrier to success is the fear of failure.'

The interesting prospect now is what you would do if you knew you couldn't fail. That's a real green light.

The fear of success

The fear of success is, I admit, difficult to understand. We all want success in our lives, so how could we possibly fear it? We can see how the fear of failure can limit us in achieving our goals, but the fear of success appears to work in a different way. We have a goal and we are striving for it, yet the fear of reaching it holds us back. It doesn't make sense, does it?

We must examine this odd state of affairs. Perhaps your fear of success was seeded when you were a young child. You were repeatedly told that you couldn't do something. This was nothing short of brainwashing, and what you were being told became so

CIRCLE OF EXCELLENCE

1. Identify the external triggers for the unresourceful state. These could be visual, auditory, tactile, smell or taste stimuli.

2. Build a powerful resource state using the circle of excellence technique. To create a circle of excellence, draw an imaginary circle on the floor or mark a circle in chalk large enough to step into.

3. Remember experiences where you felt powerful, creative or composed, or any resourceful state where you felt balanced and centred.

4. Step into the circle only as quickly or slowly as you remember and re-access the resourceful state through your inner senses, that is, see what you saw through your own eyes within the actual experience, hear the sounds and language used, and get in touch with your posture, breathing and emotions when inside the desirable resource memory. Note that an observer would see changes in your physiology such as better posture, deeper breathing and skin colour changes. If there is no noticeable change in your physiology the resource state is either poorly accessed or of low intensity. If it is of low intensity, choose another resource state that is more powerful.

5. Repeat step 4. with an additional resource state, continuing to add resource states one at a time. When you have enough resources, you step automatically into a very powerful state on entering the circle, which is truly now a circle of excellence.

6. Recall a trigger for the unresourceful state as you step into the circle of excellence.

7. Repeat the process with each old trigger, as you step into the circle of excellence.

deeply ingrained in you that it turned into a self-fulfilling prophecy. You even indulged in self-sabotage to support this belief. Like most young people you had a goal in mind and you pulled out all the stops to achieve it. However, when your efforts started to produce results, you found all of a sudden that you didn't have the time to commit to this goal. Bizarrely you lost the drive and motivation and you put it off for another time. You told yourself this was not because it wasn't important to you but because you came too close to accomplishing it. The reasoning is odd but it's probably because you have been conditioned – or brainwashed. The reasons you give yourself are actually excuses.

All the time you were fooling yourself by trying to reach your goals, because in reality you were trying not to reach them. Then you avoided working on your goal and you reinforced the habit of procrastination. The procrastination stopped you from taking a fresh look at your goal. In short, you were afraid of success because you were wrongly convinced of your own inability. You'll never get there with this attitude. Rudyard Kipling got it in one when he wrote: 'Of all the liars in the world, sometimes the worst are your own fears.'

I believe, however, that this fear goes even further. It's not fear of success itself that is the problem but rather the fear of the side effects of success. This, I'm sure, is what your mind is telling you: 'Change is scary. I won't be the same person. People will treat me differently. People will expect me to succeed in everything. I don't deserve to be happy.' And we have to banish this kind of thinking.

Julie's heavy problem

Here is a strange story, with parallels to the description above. Julie's goal was to lose three stone. In this respect she was not unlike millions of women worldwide. Like most people she knew what she should and should not eat. She knew she should exercise too. So far her story is copybook. Julie had been on every diet imaginable. You name it. She had done the green days and the red days, she had counted calories and points, she had done the no-carb diet, the low-carb diet, the no-protein diet, the high-protein diet. She was a walking encyclopaedia of what she should do, yet nothing had worked in the long term. She had followed the usual pattern in that she had lost weight and then piled the fat back on in bucketfuls. She suffered the slimmer's disappointment of being heavier than when she started.

Julie's story is so familiar, yet there was something more, something really off-centre. When I began working with her it was clear from what she said that she had an internal conflict. She had been successful, sometimes losing two stone. But just when she was doing great something happened. She lost her motivation and slipped back into her old routine of comfort eating and eating for any reason except hunger. Why?

The she explained. She was afraid that men would find her attractive if she lost the weight! Most girls would shriek with laughter at that one. Men would approach her and she might even end up in a relationship, she said. Provided the right man comes along surely that's what every heterosexual young woman wants. However, Julie expressed her fears with horror, as if meeting Mr Right was the worst thing in the world. She told me she had once been married for ten years and that her husband had treated her very badly. I won't give any grisly details, but suffice it to say he had done a real job on her. The trauma of being married to him was that she was petrified of ever dating again. This cruel man had done unforgivable damage to Julie. Part of her wanted to lose weight to feel better about herself, to feel more attractive to herself and healthier. The other part of her, the wounded part, was afraid. She feared that if she felt more attractive to herself she would be more attractive to others, and she certainly didn't want that.

Julie was also worried that her girlfriends would treat her differently, perhaps seeing her as a threat. They might think she was just not the same Julie. She feared she would lose them and they were all she had.

She needed to look seriously at her feelings, to understand them and to get them in order. The Swiss psychologist Carl Jung put it somewhat poetically: 'Your vision will become clear only when you can look into your own heart. Who looks outside dreams. Who looks inside awakes.'

I used a technique integrating Julie's conflicting parts. It enabled Julie to open up a dialogue between the two conflicting parts. She used the resources from both to create a solution and then integrated the two parts to create a whole. The long and the short of it was that she could fix her eyes on her goal without the old conflict. She settled her concerns and found a resolution she was happy with. Today Julie's story is a joyful one, not a strange one. She has lost the three stone and has kept trim for more than two years. She is happy with herself and her life and she no longer uses food as a shield. How many on-off-on flab-fighters could learn to look at themselves as Julie did and find the lurking cause of their problems?

PUTTING IT ALL IN PERSPECTIVE

This letter is reprinted from Robert Cialdini's book *Influence*:

Dear Mother and Dad

Since I left for college I have been remiss in writing and I am sorry for my thoughtlessness in not having written before. I will bring you up to date now, but before you read on, please sit down, okay?

Well, then, I am getting along pretty well now. The skull fracture and the concussion I got when I jumped out of the window of my dormitory when it caught on fire shortly after my arrival here is pretty well healed now. I only spent two weeks in the hospital and now I can see almost normally and only get those sick headaches once a day. Fortunately, the fire in the dormitory, and my jump, were witnessed by an attendant at the gas station near the dorm, and he was the one who called the fire department and the ambulance. He also visited me in the hospital and since I had nowhere to live because of the burnt-out dormitory, he was kind enough to invite me to share his apartment with him. It's really a basement room, but it's kind of cute. He is a very fine boy, and we have fallen deeply in love and are planning to get married. We haven't set the exact date yet, but it will be before my pregnancy begins to show.

Yes, Mother and Dad, I am pregnant. I know how much you are looking forward to being grandparents and I know you will welcome the baby and give it the same love and devotion and tender care you gave me when I was a child. The reason for our delay in marriage is that my boyfriend has a minor infection which prevents us from passing our premarital blood tests and I carelessly caught it from him. I know that you will welcome him into our family with open arms. He is kind and, although not well educated, he is ambitious.

Now that I have brought you up to date, I want to tell you that there was no dormitory fire, I did not have a concussion or skull fracture, I was not in hospital, I am not pregnant, I am not engaged, I am not infected, and there is no boyfriend. However, I am getting a D in American history and an F in chemistry, and I want you to see those marks in their proper perspective.

Your loving daughter

Sharon

CHAPTER 27

Resources all around

I had the great honour of delivering a seminar on getting the most out of your mind to a group of highly trained military servicemen who specialise in going into extreme situations at the drop of a hat. It was an experience that taught me things I had never even thought about and told me something about the use of resources. Every one of the group was a survival expert and capable of making it in places from the desert to the Antarctic. During the seminar one of the topics I talked about was using the mind's resources to get from where you are to where you want to be.

After the seminar I was talking to one of the sergeants. As I said before, the most revealing exchanges often happen outside the formal meeting. The sergeant, obviously fascinated by resources, told me how interesting he found the talk. Then he went into detail about the men's training. He said that among the many things they learn is how to make a fire in any condition without a lighter or matches. You have to use whatever resources are available.

He was beginning to make me curious, so I said: 'Show me.' Quick and willing to oblige, the sergeant took some anti-freeze and some potassium permanganate and poured a little into some newspaper. The newspaper started smoking, the sergeant blew on it and flames appeared. He then poured some potassium permanganate on the floor and took a boiled sweet. He crushed the sweet with the back of his knife and rubbed it into smaller pieces. He explained that the sugar from the sweet would generate a spark and so it did. Again a flame appeared. He made a spark with a flint on some pine shavings and they began to burn. He said the pine shavings had a natural turpentine, which is of course flammable. He continued in this vein and within ten minutes he had demonstrated more than ten ways to light a fire depending on the resources. He emphasised that there are always resources that you can use. You just have to know where to look for them. He said: 'That's just what you were saying, wasn't it?' I smiled back at him.

Yes, he had illustrated the points I had been making in the formal part of the seminar. The only difference is that you have millions of resources already inside you, compared with about ten ways to light a fire. There were times when you were confident, times when you achieved things, times when you used a strategy to get you to places in a different context. Every time you were using resources inside you. The good book says wisely: 'Seek and ye shall find.'

There's a huge store to draw on, one into which you delved when you stopped smoking. In all circumstances you have to refine your search. So ask yourself the following:

- What resources do I require to achieve my goal?
- What resources do I already have that I can use to achieve my goal?
- What resources do I require that I can learn from others?
- How can I utilise previously overlooked opportunities outside the box?

So let's finish this section where we began, with an idea. This book, for example, started as an idea. If it had been left as just an idea, I might never have begun. However, I took action, refining my concept and asking empowering questions. I had powerful reasons that upheld my belief that I could do the book. And here we are. This chapter was written, along with all the others, but I had the concept to start the book. From little acorns . . .

I can assure you that sometimes raw reasoning gets in the way of achievement. So suspend your pragmatic and logical disbelief for a while and just allow yourself to dream. You can dream about ideas that inspire you, dream about the things you want and the things you can have. As you float in this little fantasy heaven of yours take the ideas on board. They will become seeds that will begin to grow,

ACTION PLAN FOR YOUR ROUTE MAP

WHAT CAN I DO TODAY TO TAKE THE FIRST STEP?

WHAT CAN I DO THIS WEEK?

WHAT CAN I DO THIS MONTH?

WHAT CAN I DO NEXT MONTH?

WHAT DO I WANT TO HAVE ACHIEVED BY THE END OF THIS YEAR?

given the right water and food. The process would be like the growing of a tree. Nobody knows exactly how the tree will grow, and that makes its progress more exciting. At first its roots begin to take hold and soon the plant reaches the surface. The tree grows towards the sun and is shaped by the wind and the environment. As it becomes strong the tree bears fruit and seeds. The seeds fall off and begin to grow and in due course from one tree a forest is sprung.

You can liken the development of your concept with the growth of the tree. When we become fully committed to the concept it becomes stronger and bears fruit.

However, genuine commitment is vital. Try this little test with a trusted friend. Stand upright with one arm extended horizontally to one side. Ask your friend to try to push it down as you repeat something that is clearly and demonstrably true. For example, say: 'Today is Tuesday.' Provided the day is Tuesday, of course! Your arm will remain rigid. That is because you are telling the truth. Now repeat this exercise, but this time with an obvious lie. Declare: 'I have 15 first class university degrees.' Your arm will be pushed down easily. I assume that you haven't got those 15 degrees!

Here is another interesting point, though it is a little-known fact. You may have learnt it at school when you memorised the colours of the rainbow. No two people anywhere in the world can see the same rainbow! Even the slightest difference in height or viewpoint means that you see the colours of refracted light from different drops of moisture. Therefore, what you see is different from what the man in the next street sees and from what President George Bush sees in Washington. So it is with everything in life. 'To different minds, the same world is a hell, and a heaven,' wrote Ralph Waldo Emerson, the American essayist and poet and leader of the Transcendentalist movement. It is important to keep this in mind because it tells us that every other soul on this planet has an outlook on life that is different from yours. In the print world, interestingly, Pantone numbers are given to coloured inks to make sure that a specific shade is used. How sensible. One man's vision of bright red, for example, may not be what the person next to him sees as bright red.

Those two examples have their basis in the laws of physics and optometry. In the wider world there are many more subtle variations of outlook. This is because they are influenced by people's experience, ethos, nature and nurture. Another eminent commentator on life, the British wartime leader Winston Churchill, put it graphically: 'The optimist sees opportunity in every danger. The pessimist sees danger in every opportunity.'

I offer you another illustration. When the January temperature reaches minus 20 degrees Celsius a resident of Winnipeg would think: 'It's milder today.' Somebody living in London would have the same thought if the temperature was at least 10 degrees Celsius. A difference of opinion? Hardly. The only differences are the normal environments and the outlooks of the two people concerned.

To a grandmother driving her car on the motorway 50mph might seem fast. To the teenager in his dad's sports car, who is trying to get past the dear old soul, anything under 80mph is slow. The environment and road conditions are similar. Only the two drivers' outlooks are different.

Albert Einstein puts matters on a broader canvas. He once said: 'There are two ways to live. You can live as if nothing is a miracle. You can live as if everything is a miracle.' The choice is yours, just as the choice was yours when you quit smoking.

I recall a story that was doing the rounds at sales seminars a few years ago. It was the tale of a salesman who was sent to a remote part of Africa to open up the market for training shoes.

After a week of fact-finding he sent an e-mail to his New York headquarters. You may think his report was predictably negative. 'Coming home,' he said, 'entire population runs around barefooted, this market not even worth considering.' On the face of it, the salesman's reaction was pretty reasonable. However, the representative of a rival company went to the same bare-foot territory. This one, however, was more of a live wire. His e-mail said: 'Ship out full range immediately and consider opening local factory. Vast untapped market as nobody has any shoes.' That's initiative for you. Same environment, similar products, but different outlooks.

Try this for the effects of differing outlooks. If you have to return a faulty product to a shop, you will feel understandably miffed. Your instinct may be to charge back to the store, throw the goods on the counter and give the nearest hapless assistant the tongue-lashing of his life. But, steady on, reflect before you rage. Put yourself in the assistant's position for a moment and you will see how unfair it is that he is being blamed for a cock-up in quality control at a factory in China. Don't you think you're going for the wrong target *and* creating a barrier of hostility between you and the shop? Instead of storming in like a demented typhoon, talk calmly, quietly and politely. Begin with: 'I need your help, please, because . . . ' Then explain the facts. Forget your own feelings and emotions for as long as takes to get a result. Hitting the roof is not good for your blood pressure anyway!

When you have even the briefest relationship with another human, such as the till girl in a supermarket checkout, your outlooks will be different. If you want to achieve anything in life you must think of the long term. Along the way you must be aware of other people's outlooks if things are to run smoothly.

Story time again. A man found a butterfly cocoon. One day a small opening appeared, and the man sat and watched the butterfly for several hours as it struggled to force its body through the hole. Then it seemed to stop making any progress. The butterfly appeared to have progressed as far as it could and could go no further.

Then the man decided to help the butterfly, but this was his big mistake. He took a pair of scissors and snipped the remaining part of the cocoon. He thought he had done the right thing because the butterfly then slid out easily. But something was strange. The butterfly had a swollen body and shrivelled wings. The man continued to watch the butterfly because he expected that at any moment the wings would enlarge and expand to support the body, and that the body would contract in time. Neither happened. In fact, the butterfly spent the rest of its life miserably crawling around with a swollen body and deformed wings. It was never able to fly. Big mistake with the scissors.

Our man's good intentions coupled with ignorance had put a curse on the butterfly. He had his own outlook and own human model of the world, but they were not right for the butterfly. He had not realised that the restricting cocoon and the struggle required for the butterfly to get through the small opening were nature's way of forcing fluid from its body and into its wings. If left alone the butterfly would have been ready for flight once it had broken free from the cocoon.

You've often heard it said that you cherish something more because you've had to work hard for it. Sometimes what appears to be a struggle is exactly what we need in our life. If we were allowed to go through life without any obstacles, that would cripple us. We would not be as strong as we could have been. Not only that, we could never fly. The Latin phrase, *per aspera ad astra*, the motto of Nasa, the American space agency, means: 'We go through hardships to reach the stars.' It's applicable to all of us who strive to achieve anything.

You will rapidly establish rapport and a good relationship with others when you endeavour to see the reality of a situation from their perspective. This does not mean you have to allow them to walk all over your opinion but, just for a while, you should recognise that they have a different angle. Step into their shoes. It may be helpful to remember the old saying that you should never judge a man until you have walked a mile in his moccasins. It is thought to be American Indian in its origin and it has several variants. Wherever it comes from, it's so true.

Experience, too, the almost magical power of 'because'. There will invariably be times when you need to jump a queue for some perfectly valid reason. To everybody else waiting patiently in line you will seem to be a dislikeable ignoramus who barges in. So, instead of blundering insensitively past all those people, temporarily take on their outlook and say: 'Do you mind if I go in front of you because . . .?' Then follow up with a brief and valid reason. Believe it or not, they will usually be happy to surrender their place. It pays to think how *you* would feel in their situation and adjust your approach accordingly. Be ready, naturally, for the occasional coarse character who gives you a mouthful and invites you to shove off.

Time means different things to different people. Although we all have the same 24 hours in a day, every individual has a different outlook on time. Our particular outlook changes even according to our circumstances. On holiday, a week or two can just fly by as we relax and have fun. Back home, when we are waiting for a bus or train a mere 20-minute delay can seem to last for ever. If we are already running late for an appointment, every minute can feel like an hour. You may be in a rush, but a little understanding is called for here. The people delaying you in traffic or in a queue may not be so pressed for time. Instead of working yourself into a needless lather of hypertension, just accept that their outlook is different and move on as soon as you can. Be logical if possible. Your impatience will neither alter the facts nor get you to where you want to be any sooner.

Be a little caring too and step into those other people's shoes. Rein in your impatient outbursts because your outlook can, and does, affect those around you. This is at the very heart of making contagious changes. There is no need to take my word for this, as you will have ample experiences to refer to. When you have been with somebody who is close to you emotionally but who is also depressed, miserable and full of self-pity and gloom, you will have been left feeling equally ground down. A bit of a drag, isn't it? But when you have been with others who are happy, optimistic and full of enthusiasm and fun, you will have been given a lift. If their outlook affects you, yours can affect them. Appreciating this can be another way of stepping outside the box.

Say no to no

Better still, don't let negative thinking or fear determine your mood. I know it's easy to say that but another example that rings a bell with most of us makes the point. Every driver knows that the sight of flashing blue lights in the rear view mirror can provoke a swift but thorough examination of conscience, coinciding with an empty feeling in the pit of the stomach. You fear the worst. This gut-twisting instantly turns to relief when the boys in blue flash past and pay no attention to you.

You may assume that the officers are late for the end of their shift and are hightailing it back to the nick. Or you may spend the rest of your journey wondering when you are going to come across wrecked vehicles. Those are just two ways of interpreting the same facts. It may be mischievous to think this way, but if you had a fast white car with candy-coloured stripes, relative immunity from prosecution, and blue flashers, you might enjoy hightailing it along the highway too!

I want to believe you are reading this book because you have chosen to take a journey to success. Of course, you could have no wish to make any more changes and are just reading out of idle curiosity. You have at least two options for interpreting any situation. You can look for the positive and then power your journey forward, or you can wallow in the negative and go nowhere. Think back, however. You were positive when you decided to stop smoking, and that was worth the effort, wasn't it? Any consideration of the N-word must take into account that some people simply enjoy being negative. Without even realising it, they have befriended negativity and decided that the pay-off has some value in it.

Listen to George Foreman, the former world heavyweight boxing champion. He says: 'I let that negativity roll off me like water off a duck's back. If it's not positive, I didn't hear it.'

Others choose not to be positive. So what is this fabulous pay-off that entraps them? The most common attitude is that, if you always expect the worst, you can never be disappointed when your dreams don't come true. Then you say you never really believed in them anyway. However, this attitude can be like a progressive illness. The next step is that you stop dreaming anyway as you drift around your grey world of uniformity. You expect everybody to let you down. That's a stage further than being prepared for disappointment and it's a sad frame of mind. You may even imagine that your headache from watching too much television is the onset of a fatal tumour and, probably, you will end your days prematurely. You will have spread gloom and doom throughout your life. And that really *is* contagious.

This doesn't have to happen. It is a basic law of physics that every force has an equal and opposite force. So now consider the force that is opposite to negativity.

You may know this force as PMA, standing for Positive Mental Attitude. Now you must not confuse it with PMT, as any woman will tell you! PMA will result in a totally different frame of mind from the attitude of that gloomy cove. However, before we wave farewell to those negative souls above, consider their take on PMA. They will accuse you of living in cloud-cuckoo-land, of building castles in the air, of being a daydream believer and of doing a passable impression of an ostrich with its head in the sand. The N-word really does apply to them and they could drag you into a depression. If you fit all of their descriptions, they must imagine you have PMA oozing from every pore. To them you will appear to be one of those magical people who actually manage to do something with your back to the wall, your nose to the grindstone, your shoulder to the wheel and your best foot forward. There are some good descriptions for you. Take them as compliments. If you don't let the Jeremiahs cast a blanket over you, then you must be succeeding.

The pay-off to PMA is that you will enjoy every moment of your life as it unfolds. We've already talked of how you can affect people around you with your emotional state. As a PMA person you will add brightness and lightness to others. You will wake up most mornings with a zest for creating something great in the next 24 hours. Guess what? You will dare to dream big, and those dreams that are within your mental and physical capabilities will come true. If you follow that equal and opposite rule, this too is powerfully contagious. Never doubt that positive force.

Vernon Howard, who taught and wrote about remedies to human suffering, was a sworn enemy of negativity. He said: 'Quit thinking that you must halt before the barrier of inner negativity. You need not. You can crash through . . . whatever we see a negative state, that is where we can destroy it.'

That's a fine principle to observe in life, though it is true that even with a great PMA you will still experience the odd bad-hair day. It's part of being a human being. But there is good news. These down times do pass quickly and they become infrequent because you know, deep within, that they always have evaporated previously and that they will flee again. It is said that 'into every life some rain must fall'. And of course that rain is a must. If we never had rain we would have no crops, orchards or lakes, and we would appreciate the warm summer sunshine less. Bear in mind, too, that the stuff that pours from your bathroom shower and kitchen taps would be more expensive than gold. You can regard the down times, therefore, as having a purpose. When you stopped smoking there were probably difficult days, but you felt so much better after you got through them.

It comes down to this. You have a choice. You can choose to see your world in shades of grey, or you can mentally flip the page to see it in wide-screen colour with dynamic surround sound. Am I being naïve in saying there is a choice? Come on, in reality this is no choice. Why settle for less than the world has to offer? You would be squiffy if you didn't want all the good things around you.

As you affirm, so it will be. This quote comes from the works of Emile Coué, a French pioneer of hypnosis, who lived from 1857 to 1926. As a psychologist and psychotherapist he was a great advocate of the power of affirmations. Coué's take on affirmations is that by their constant repetition they will become etched into you and you will be guided to take the actions that make them happen. Coué's favourite affirmation was: 'Every day, and in every way, I am becoming better and better.'

Do a little recapping and ask these questions:

- Do you consider yourself to be a negative or a positive person?
- Do you immediately see the worst of every situation, or the best?
- Do you see a glass as half-empty or half-full?
- Do you look forward to the future with dire dread or cheerful optimism?
- Do you believe that the good old days were then, or that the best is yet to come?
- Do you consider yourself unlucky or lucky?

Everybody has that choice, to wallow in the minuses of life or to spurn negativity and embrace PMA. The more you practise, the better you will become, and very soon you will become a positive person.

But beware the propaganda you impose on yourself. Negativity will pervade every cell of your being if you give it half a chance. And don't assume that it means only being miserable. Negative people tend to have a weaker immune system, and that makes them more susceptible to whatever virus is flying about. Look around you at the bright and breezy souls you know. Aren't they generally fit and well in addition to being happy? That's right, positive people have fewer ailments and recover faster.

Yes, a positive outlook has a beneficial impact on every area of your life.

Self-starters

The only true and lasting motivation is self-motivation.

Analyse self-motivation and you see it is powered by the prevention of pain and the pursuit of pleasure.

Those two short lines contain the most common reasons why even the best-intentioned goals can fail to deliver. So how can you ensure that you do not fall into the flawed motivation trap?

First, you must take on board the concept of self-motivation. Do you remember we determined that any target you are aiming at must be for you, not directly for anybody else? When you decided to stop smoking it had to be for you first and foremost. You must not do something because somebody else wants you to do it, but because *you* want to.

Every action, without exception, produces a result or outcome. When you focus strongly on that result, you will be strongly self-motivated to do whatever it takes to get there.

We'll start with the prevention of pain. This is a negative, but powerful motivator. It gets you going when you realise you have to take action to avoid an uncomfortable situation deteriorating further. For example, if you do not pay your telephone bill, you will be cut off and then incur a fee for the service to be resumed. That's the penalty you pay for being sluggish or tight-fisted about stumping up. So, although it may be annoying and inconvenient to settle the bill, you are motivated to do it if you wish to avoid the even greater pain of inconvenience and higher costs.

Now we come to the pursuit of pleasure. It's an equally powerful motivator but it's a positive driver. I don't actually need to give examples of this as you can think of many of your own pleasurable experiences. Do you remember the excitement you felt when you looked forward to a special outing or holiday? You were motivated to plan, to make the booking and to pack your bags for this jolly. Maybe you even counted down the days. Perhaps your childhood memories of this kind of happy feeling are the most vivid. Well ahead of time out came the bucket and spade and the swimming gear, and all the childish chatter.

Of course, pain need not be physical, like toothache. It can more often be mental pain and its characteristics are unusually high stress levels and depression. Similarly, pleasure need not mean a material reward. This too can be mental. It can be the great feeling you have when you know you have done something to perfection. You get that proud glow of achievement.

At any time you will be travelling somewhere along this motivational line:

Pain _____   _____Pleasure
                    Mind The Gap!

The progression and regression along this line are interesting. As you move away from the feelings, sensation or fear of pain you must, obviously, head towards pleasure. You are motivated at the outset to shift rapidly away from the source of pain. Then, as the pain diminishes with distance, your motivation diminishes too. However now the alarm bells should be ringing. You are close to the danger point. Unless you have a strong vision of your ultimate pleasure, that motivation can fall 'through the gap'. It wanes or disappears altogether, and that, sadly, is a very human trait. The normal result of this is that you drift back towards the pain end of the line and the cycle is repeated.

This game of tag doesn't have to happen. The three fuels of self-motivation are focus, repetition and enthusiasm. As you repeatedly review your goal and take action, maintain your focus on the end result, which is the pleasure, and keep positive and enthusiastic about what you are achieving along the way. Keep the ball rolling away from the pain station.

You can use this next step to strengthen your resolve after you've decided to stop smoking and you can adapt it for any other significant goal in your life. Draw up a scale of 0 to 10, in which 0 indicates 'not at all enthusiastic' and 10 stands for 'bursting with enthusiasm'. What is your present level of enthusiasm for being a non-smoker? You must be honest on a matter of such importance to your well-being.

If your score is 6 or lower, ask yourself: 'What would it take to score 7 or higher?' I make the point because any goal that has an enthusiasm rating below 7 will stand little chance of being achieved. Would-be non-smokers should think long and hard about that.

The higher your enthusiasm score, the better your chances of ultimate success. To raise a low score, you have to create a new set of goals that will allow you to answer the question about what it would take to hit 7.

You may answer: "I do not know.' Then the clincher question is: 'If you did know, what do you think that answer would be?'

Try this secondary clincher question: 'What information do I have to acquire so that I would know the answer?'

Changing all the time

There's another way of looking at changing yourself. Did you realise you were already transforming? Silently, you are undergoing a transformation literally all the time. I expect your sense of taste is highly important to you. Did you know that was constantly changing? There are 26,000 taste buds in your mouth and every two to three days they are completely replaced. The change doesn't stop there. Every month your body quietly works away to create a whole new layer of skin cells, and every seven years your body completely changes every cell and every fibre. So seven years from now you'll be wearing a totally new body. A frightening thought! That's the physiological transformation that's happening. So why can't you have a total transformation internally and externally?

Be assured you can transform your life. I really must hammer home this message to be certain that you get it. The most important word is 'you'. Yes, you. Not your spouse, partner, lover, pet goldfish or your favourite bare-footed, long-haired, pot-smoking, gong-banging guru. Now jump to the last two words of that sentence, 'your life'. It must be yours, not somebody else's, and it must be life, not existence. The actor Will Smith said the memorable words in the film *Hitch*: 'Life is not the amount of breaths you take. It's the moments that take your breath away.'

Be brutally frank again now. If you can honestly state that everything in your life, without exception, is exactly the way that you want it to be and that you have absolute happiness, then that's fantastic. Arthur Rubinstein, one of the 20th century's greatest pianists, said something like that as he looked back over his life. He died at 95, presumably very happy. That sort of euphoria doesn't often happen, does it? More often it's a case of TOT, meaning triumph over tragedy. Individuals, dissatisfied with what fate has handed them, have literally transformed their lives. We both know that they exist and you may even have first-hand experience. For now I want to fast-forward to the point of transformation.

Heed the words of Wes Nisker, the American exponent of Buddhist meditation: 'Any revolution has to start with the transformation of the individual; otherwise individuals are corrupted by the power they get if their revolution succeeds.'

You may prefer to think of it as re-inventing yourself, though, being pernickety, one is inclined to ask how something can be re-invented once it has been invented!

Transformation can be quite a journey. Some fascinating insights and discoveries can be found on that journey if you are open to them. Think of the electricity transformer that we all know. It changes electrical energy into a state in which it can be used.

There is a charming story in *Perfume of the Desert: Inspirations from Sufi Wisdom*, by Andrew Harvey and Eryk Hanut: 'A man was chased off a cliff by a tiger. He fell, and just managed to hold on to a branch. Six feet above him stood the tiger, snarling. A hundred feet below, a violent sea lashed fierce-looking rocks. To his horror, he noticed that the branch he was clutching was being gnawed at its roots by two rats. Seeing he was doomed, he cried out: "O Lord, save me!" He heard a Voice reply: "Of course, I will save you. But first, let go of the branch."'

Back to the self-starting message. You must not depend on others to transform you. By all means use their skills, talents and abilities to fill any gaps in your own knowledge or experience, but the bottom line is that you must constantly remind yourself that you are the master or mistress of your own destiny. Your mantra must be: 'If it is to be, it is up to me.' Repeat this mantra daily, on the hour, every hour!

Go with it

The transformation of which you are capable is practically endless. You can even change what you do, say or think about others. That might seem a problem for some but it really is quite easy to make those adjustments. But don't get carried away. It's virtually impossible to change others who see nothing amiss with their conduct or attitude and do not *want* to change. Do you see what I mean about everything being down to you?

The crucial words for change are 'want to'. You will inevitably encounter folk who behave in a manner that either stresses or distresses you. As you must know unless you've been living in a museum all your days, life is not always pink and fluffy. These difficult types are always popping up to bug you. If you stand up to them, you may win, but more frequently you won't even dent their attitudes and ideas. Acceptance is the ultimate answer that allows you to stay on course with the wonderful life that you have decided to create for yourself, even when it suffers a glancing blow from these individuals. However, there are other ways of dealing with those awkward characters.

First, consider the option of avoidance. If you can reduce the frequency of adverse encounters it's wise do so. Don't give yourself the grief of having to deal with people you dislike. Better still, if you can totally avoid the circumstances that involve contact with such people, it's even wiser – though it may mean a change of routine, job or, in extreme cases, spouse. Again, weigh up the costs and benefits on a balance sheet.

Before we go any further, please realise that the concept of acceptance does not turn you into a human doormat. On the contrary, that submissive frame of mind is out of bounds. It's alien to the new you. You must not even think of adopting a victim attitude if you are powerless. Instead, seek the outcomes in which you can be a victor with a range of options open to you.

Acceptance simply means you do not *react* to these people who may not agree with your views. You accept they are that way, that it is their style and that they are probably doing the best they know to get through life with the experience and tricks available to them. But you must not allow them to influence you. The key is to let them get on with it, with no resistance from you. Accept that you cannot change them. Accept at the same time that you can usually ignore them and can certainly refuse to get involved in their mind games or devious manoeuvres.

The alternative is dangerous. If you opt in and play along with them, you implicitly endorse their behaviour and they will continue to think it is OK by you. Acquiescence is hardly different from acting like a doormat.

Acceptance without endorsement is the only sensible way. When somebody tries to push or pull you in a particular direction, your instinct will be to resist. It's natural enough but it's a mug's game. A battle of wits and brawn results, in which the harder you resist, the harder your adversary will persist. What a waste of time and effort! The persistence and resistance will sap your mental and physical energies and distract you from your own aims, goals and objectives. Eventually the strongest will prevails, but what was the point? What have you gained?

Don't assume that you must have a view on everything, whatever you feel when somebody expresses an opinion aggressively and clearly wants a good ding-dong. You know the type. He stands in front of you with confrontation written all over his face. You're a challenge, but don't give him the satisfaction. He may be defying you to argue, but your best hand is to stand down with quiet defiance. It is perfectly OK not to have an opinion and, even if you do have one, it is often better to keep it to yourself when face to face with someone who delights in scoring points. The more you resist, the more strongly your opponent will persist. Ask yourself what is to be gained by sustained resistance.

When you stop resisting, through your passive acceptance, the other party no longer has anything to push or pull against. This leaves him with such a meaningless and frustrating endeavour that he soon gives up and looks for another victim. Your policy is the best one because the result, which you wanted anyway, is that you come out the victor.

Acceptance is such a useful tool. You can apply it to events, feelings and circumstances too. It is especially handy in the workplace. Getting hacked off about an unexpected and unwanted demand to work overtime will only make the task harder, so accept that it has to be done and do it with good grace. As a pal of mine once quipped, if good Grace isn't available, see whether she has a friend who can help you! Levity aside, if you feel angry, fearful, hurt or miserable, accept that such feelings are normal and be assured they will soon pass, as they always have before. The more you resist them, the longer they will prevail. If you are stuck in a traffic jam you can induce hypertension, hyperplasia, dyspepsia and a whole load of other medical conditions with similar names by getting het up, anxious or angry. Accept that nothing that you do is going to make a tad of difference to the snarl-up. Instead, chill out by listening to a mellow music station on the car audio.

The very next time, and every time from then on, that you find yourself resisting anything, ask yourself these three questions:

1. Could I let this go and accept it? The answer is always yes. Of course you *could* if you wanted to!
2. Would I let this go and accept it? If not, you'd better have a damned good reason!
3. When? What's the point of prolonging the agony of resistance?

If the answer to 3 is not 'now', then ask yourself this further question: 'When will now be a good time?'

CHAPTER 28

Giving is receiving

Great to get gifts, isn't it? There is a small part of all of us that has not moved on since childhood. The thrill we had as children tearing off the wrapping paper on Christmas morning has remained. It's one of the more delightful aspects of life. The chances are that you probably get even more pleasure from gifts that arrive unexpectedly and at unexpected times. It is also a paradox of life that the more you give the more you will receive.

If you're sceptical about that, consider why I say it. If your life is full to the brim, there is no room for anything else to be accommodated. As soon as you create a little clear space by giving, then you have room to receive. The equation is quite straightforward.

Despite what your ever-loving Mummy and Daddy may have told you as a child, value is not always measured in terms of what you have in your wallet, purse or bank. I must add, of course, that not all parents give their children this crude materialistic propaganda. Whatever your parents told you, the value of a gift is in the intention. Caring parents would have given you that message. That is why a birthday card, drawn in lurid wax crayon on the back of a cereal packet by a four-year-old, can bring a tear to the eye. It will probably be kept for ever, long after the expensively printed gold-foil card from Harrods has been recycled into . . . a cereal packet!

The clumsily drawn birthday card, worth nothing monetarily, is a gift of great value. There are other highly valuable gifts that are even less tangible. They are love, time, talents and experience and they cannot be bought at any price. But they can, and should, be freely given. When you give, with absolutely no hidden agenda or expectation of reward, you will get back more than you gave. You may doubt that statement if you take the usual consumerist attitude and see nothing physically handed back to you. However, the return may not come from the recipient of your gifts. It may come via an indirect route and it may take its time getting to you. And, it will seek out and find you, often at the time of your greatest need.

Some hard facts have to be appreciated first, of course. In our materialistic Western world you clearly need to use your time, talents and experience to earn a living so that you can pay for the necessities of life. Few of us can escape these money-centred activities. However, when you have some time left over, that is when you give. A few people argue against this idea, saying you should give first, and then you will find you always have some time left over. Be idealistic if you wish, but don't expect much sympathy from the bank manager when you use this as a reason for not reducing your overdraft, or from the taxman when you are late filing a return.

If you are giving, whether it is something material or otherwise, give because you want to, not because it makes you feel good, although it will. Give, not out of pity, piety or condescension, but out of a genuine desire to share. You've heard the words 'want to' earlier in this book. The same applies.

Most of you wouldn't have a problem finding a suitable recipient for your generosity. If in doubt, consider those that have benefited you most in the past. Is there some way that you can return part of what you have to broadly similar individuals or organisations? Here's a good example. If one particular teacher set you on a career path that has exceeded your wildest expectations, then give to an educational charity. In other words, keep the stuff flowing in the same ball park.

Giving is a many-splendoured thing. To those who have an aversion to the super-rich in society let me say I know of several millionaires who swear by the tithing concept. They give the first 10 per cent of everything they receive. When they do this, they seem to accumulate more. They say that when they miss a round of giving, things start to go a little iffy. I am not suggesting that if you are at or below the poverty level you should give a tenth of your state benefit to the first beggar who accosts you. It's only right and sensible to ensure that you have enough to support yourself and your family, but then you can forgo that luxury item you were planning to buy and give the equivalent of the price to someone in need. Instead of performing the beer-into-water miracle at your favourite pub, consider giving those hours of your time to working in a hospice or for a voluntary service.

Giving is also a test of humility because the best gifts of all are given anonymously.

Then there is the saying that is so old that it has whiskers on it: 'Give and you shall receive.'

Remember the story about the four-year-old's home-made birthday card? Some of the most welcome gifts have zero financial value. In the same vein we can all find time, talent and love to give. But be warned that this can become difficult because such gifts act like boomerangs. The more you give the more you get, and then you want to give more. Figure that one out. It is part of the answer to those who expect something in the shape of banknotes in return for their generosity. It's a shallow man or woman who measures everything in cash terms.

The essentials are that, whenever possible, you should give anonymously and always with *no* expectation of a return. Give the best you can and never ask: 'What's in it for me?'

If you have the right attitude your generosity will carry a health warning: 'Giving, like smiling, is contagious in the extreme.'

Knock, knock

Do you hate it when people talk about opportunities? Do you feel that opportunity just does not knock at your door? This sounds glib, but it would help if you had a door knocker and actually answered the door sometimes. If the road to hell is paved with good intentions, may I hazard the suggestion that the road to success can have speed humps of lost opportunities?

So do you also hate it when people talk about lost opportunities? Like anything else that is lost, an opportunity has to exist before it can be lost or found. Alas, despite the plethora of get-rich-quick 'opportunities' to be found in every weekly issue of *Exchange & Mart*, there is no warehouse of wholesale opportunities that you can visit. So you ask where you can find them. Fair enough?

The answer is that, like ideas, opportunities can be found anywhere and everywhere. It's the lively enterprising mind that spots them and grabs them. You may wonder at this but Coca-Cola could have gone down the drain but for a live wire with imagination. Coca-Cola, now one of the world's best-known brands, started life as a failed indigestion and headache cure. Hard to believe, isn't it? As the company smarted from its disappointment somebody spotted the opportunity to market the product as a soft drink, and the rest is history.

I expect everybody has used Post-it Notes without giving a thought to their background. Those little pieces of paper represent a failed attempt to find a new adhesive. The project failed because the adhesive lost its stickiness after a while. Many would have thrown the whole idea in the bin. However, instead of discarding it, the 3M company recognised a potential opportunity and set their research and development department the task of creating a use for it. Now millions of those little packs are in use around the world. I'll bet you're going to ask why Post-its are always yellow! Sorry, no idea. Perhaps there is an opportunity for somebody to create chrome and gold effect versions for the 'chav and bling' market.

If I mention Bernard Matthews you will automatically hear the word 'bootiful' and start to salivate. You might not immediately think of his thriving business as a revolution. People had been raising turkeys for generations in Britain, depending on Christmas and Easter for the bulk of their trade. But the turkey business made Matthews think. If turkey was popular wasn't there an opportunity to market turkey meat in different forms as a year-round product? He scooped up the opportunity and became very wealthy. Matthews was good news too for a lot of others. Many of the farmers supplying the Matthews factory are also becoming wealthy.

The good ideas don't always flow from the big organisations. Many small business ventures have been built on the opportunities that fall like crumbs from the tables of the big players. It's another way of thinking big. Several management consultancies, advertising agencies and accountancy practices have been started by entrepreneurs who realised they could earn significant income by serving the low-capital end market that the megabuck agencies couldn't even consider because of their high overheads.

There are similar stories in publishing. White Ladder Press is a book publisher that Ros Jay started because as an author she was fed up with being regarded as a second-class citizen by the big companies. She believed there must be many other authors who had been treated like dirt. So she invited them to contact her. She had spotted an opportunity to do it better, and now her company is prospering.

Don't expect an opportunity always to be a blinding light on the road to Damascus. It can be an unspectacular happening. It is often said that opportunity doesn't always knock – it sometimes whispers quietly.

Back to an earlier question. Where do you find opportunities? I believe the simplest way to discover an opportunity is to look for a need and find a way to satisfy it. The next best way is to look for a need that is already being served, but to do it better and more cheaply or to extend it to a wider market.

Another tip is that you must not be a shrinking violet. You may have the best business, product or service on the planet however, unless people know that, all you will have is the best business, service or product. Nobody will want your wares if you hide them in a cupboard. So put them in the glare and let people know about them. Eventually your clients will come back to you and may even offer potential opportunities or suggestions. Some will begin with the words: 'Why don't you . . .?' Take every idea seriously. Whenever you have to refuse a valid request for *anything*, pause, take a breath and see whether maybe, just maybe, it is an opportunity in disguise. In fact, opportunity is a master of disguise, so be alert. The graveyard of missed opportunities is pretty full.

It's vital to be a bulldog and not let go. When you have grabbed an opportunity by the tail, hang on in there, because if you don't somebody else will. Your missed opportunity could be another man's route to riches.

The following little exercise could be a sickener, but it's best to regard it as therapy. Think of three opportunities that you feel you have missed. Why did you let them go? With the benefit of hindsight, what would you do differently if they presented themselves again? I say it is a therapeutic exercise because it may help you to capitalise on the next opportunity that jumps out at you.

Push back the barriers

If you are going to grasp your opportunity with both hands, you will be using less than one tenth of your brain power. No, I have *not* made an error! The human brain is a marvellous machine, yet its full potential has never been reached. Leading psychologists agree that most of us use only 10 per cent of our capabilities. This is like having a car with a top speed of 100mph but never pushing it past 10mph.

There's a simple activity that illustrates my assertion. Compare the use of the brain with the use of other parts of the body. Anyone who has ever worked out at a gym knows that muscles that are not used will eventually become unusable. Heed the warning and become a little more energetic. Progressively increasing the power of these muscles through sensible and controlled programmes creates greater flexibility, endurance and strength.

The little extra effort that you put in may give you the payback. Think of horseracing. The horse that wins a race may be worth 100 times more than the one that comes second. But, just a minute, it's not 100 times better. On the day it was just fractions of a second faster. Yet those tiny slices of time made a big quantum difference.

Now here is a staggering thought. Imagine what you could do if you used just a small amount of that 90 per cent 'spare' capacity in your brain. That would make a huge difference to your life. The opportunities there are almost boundless. Bringing more of your brain into play could mean the difference between just getting by and living a more meaningful life. It could mean the difference between mere existence and living an enjoyable and fulfilling life with zest, enthusiasm, optimism and happiness.

That sort of conjecture fills most people with awe. If it is so simple, you may wonder why everyone doesn't do it. It truly is this simple, but, alas, simple is not the same as easy. It's an undertaking that will take you where you've never been before. You will need to teach your mind to explore those untapped areas and this will require time and conscious effort. But you know it is well worth doing, whatever it takes. Again, I'll whisk you back to your decision to stop smoking and your subsequent action. It required new thinking and effort but you did it.

So you can begin exploring your unlimited potential with no further excuses. Just do it, and do it now.

CHAPTER 29

What does success mean to you?

Success lies at the end of the struggle. You whoop with joy when you get there. Success, however, means different things to different people. It can also mean different things to the same person, depending on focus and stage of life. For example:

At age 4, success is . . . not peeing in your pants.
At age 12, success is . . . having friends.
At age 18, success is . . . having a driver's licence.
At age 20, success is . . . having sex.
At age 35, success is . . . having money.
At age 40, success is . . . finding meaning and purpose to life.

At age 50, success is . . . having money.
At age 60, success is . . . having sex.
At age 70, success is . . . having a driver's licence.
At age 75, success is . . . having friends.
At age 80, success is . . . not peeing in your pants.

Perhaps the above list is a little simplistic or even tongue-in-cheek. But have you ever thought about what that thing you personally call success is? What makes you feel good about yourself? What makes the sun shine for you? Is it to be rich, to be famous, to be approved by people, to be loved, or maybe to be hated? Here I must observe that I am mystified how the sun can shine for somebody who strives to be hated. Yet there are those who go out of their way to offend, insult and hurt others.

The questions are not as daft as they sound because, strange as it may seem, most people never try to define their version of success. They have a disjointed picture of what they want in their mind. The picture is vague, disorganised, even half-baked, but this is the thinking that has made their lives the way they are today.

So the answer is pretty basic. You need to look hard at your internal definitions and change them to what you truly desire. If you are thinking in a practical way you can have anything you want in life. That magnificent machine inside your skull is something like a car. If you don't have control of it you will end up having a smash. But if are in control, the car makes your life easier. And so does your brain.

A quotation from Plato puts it succinctly: 'The first and best victory is to conquer self. To be conquered by self is, of all things, the most shameful and vile.' In other words, a good servant but a bad master.

Young people probably have the least disciplined idea of what they want in life. This came home to me when I asked a group of teenagers what success meant to them. To people with little experience of life this must have been a monster of a question. They gazed in open-mouthed amazement, as if I was from another planet. Although the question was new to them, they eventually came up with an answer: 'We want to be famous.' So I asked: 'Famous for what?' They had no idea. I imagined that even teenagers would have a more defined ambition than that.

Let me ask you a similar question. What is your personal definition of success? Give this some attention if you've never done it before. It matters because, until and unless you answer honestly and fully, you will not achieve success. The very first requirement for finding anything is to know what you are looking for. That's not deep philosophy. It's common sense.

However, don't expect success to come to you in a sudden whoosh. It can arrive slowly. Robert Collier, the American writer specialising in self-help, reminds us: 'Success is the sum of small efforts, repeated day in and day out.'

The key to success is focus. Don't be like those teenagers with both feet firmly planted in midair! You must have a very clear vision of what you want and train your mind to focus its power on one purpose. Co-ordinated and vigorous action towards a goal gives you the result. Looking forward to the achievement works wonders too because you know that nothing tastes as good as success feels.

But first there's work to be done. You can have the most inspiring goal in the world, the greatest of intentions and a clearly defined route map, but unless you take action you are unlikely to achieve anything. Nothing happens without action, and results follow action. Female readers will appreciate a kitchen analogy. It's like baking a chocolate cake (idea) for a dinner party (reasons). You know it's going to be the pièce de résistance of the meal (belief), you have all the ingredients (resources), and you have the recipe to follow (route map). To bring the cake to fruition you must combine all the ingredients in their correct proportions and bake the cake at the right temperature (action). You know well enough that there won't be a chocolate cake until you take action.

Dottie Walters, the public speaking trainer, once gave the following presentation, entitled *Angels Never Say Hello*:

My grandma told me about angels. She said they come knocking at the door of our hearts, trying to deliver a message to us. I saw them in my mind's eye with a big mail sack slung between their wings and a post office cap set jauntily on their head. I wondered if the stamps on their letters said Heaven Express. 'No use waiting for the angels to open your door,' grandma explained. 'You see, there is only one door handle on the door of your heart. Only one bolt. They are on the inside. Your side. You must listen for the angel, throw open the lock and open up that door!'

I loved the story and asked her again and again to tell me: 'What does the angel do then?'

'The angel never says hello, you reach out and take the message, and the angel gives you your instruction: "Arise and go forth!" Then the angel flies away. It is your responsibility to take action.'

To wind up the book, which has taken you from tobacco enslavement to fantastic achievement, let me give you a huge success story, illustrating how action turns the 'want' into a 'have'. In 1932 Ole Kirk Christiansen invented a toy for children. The plaything consisted of building blocks that when pushed together could produce a multitude of different structures and things. You could take six of his toy building blocks and find 915 million different ways to put them together. Christiansen used the principle of putting things together to name his invention. He took the first two letters of the Danish words 'leg godt', meaning 'play well', and put them together to form the word Lego. Thus Lego was born, and the ironic twist is that in Latin 'lego' means 'I bring together', and Christiansen didn't even know!

His creation of the Lego system was a metaphor for life because many thousands of building elements can be combined easily and in innumerable ways. The more Lego bricks you have the more resources you have and, to quote Lego itself, 'the more fertile your creativity can become – putting two Lego bricks together is intuitive and delivers the spontaneous joy of creation'. Just read these facts and figures for an idea of how successful Christiansen was:

- More than 400 million children and adults will play with Lego bricks this year.
- More than two million Lego bricks are manufactured every hour of every day. This figure breaks down into 33,824 every minute or 564 every second.
- On average there are 62 Lego bricks for every person on this earth.
- Approximately 400 billion Lego elements have been manufactured since 1949.

Christiansen died in 1958 to be succeeded by his son Godtfred. Christiansen Junior also inherited the success bug and was determined to build on his father's work. In 1966 he introduced the first Lego train. Numerous other innovative ideas followed and in 1977 Godtfred incorporated gears, beams and gearboxes to make movable functions. He certainly understood the principles of success, which are:

- Know your outcome.
- Take action.
- Check what is working, and what is not.
- Be flexible in your behaviour.
- Maintain a positive state.

In this book I have offered a method of stopping smoking and staying stopped, and I have pointed out a range of positive ways to live and succeed after the weed has been sent packing. I believe it would have been incomplete if all I could do was to show you a way of quitting something, however important that quitting is. Having quit, you will want to live your life in a rewarding way, and I hope I have given some pointers, whether your ambition is to go on the stage, excel at sport, build a company or become rich. Or anything else.

Edward Albee, the winner of three Pulitzer Prizes for drama, asks: 'What could be worse than getting to the end of your life and realising you hadn't lived it?' Perhaps this book will show you how you can live it.

I always love hearing about people's success with my EasyStop Method, so please email your story of triumph to me at success@easystop.co.uk

Until we meet.

Elliott

Bibliography

Bandler, R., and Grinder, J., *The structure of magic 1*, Palo Alto, Calif., 1975

Bandler, R., and Grinder, J., *The structure of magic 2*, Palo Alto, Calif., 1975

Chomsky N., *Syntactic structures*, Mouton, The Hague, 1975

Cialdini, Robert, *The New Psychology of Modern Persuasion*, New York, 1985

De Bono, Edward, *Breaking out of the Box*, Headline Book, 2001

Dilts, Robert, *From Coach to Awakener*, Meta Publications, 2003

Jarvis, M. J., *Why People Smoke*, British Medical Journal, 328

Maltz, Maxwell, *Psycho-Cybernetics*, North Hollywood, Calif., 1973

Neil, Michael, *You Can Have What You Want*, Hay House, 2006

Poitier, Sidney, *The Measure of a Man*, Simon and Schuster, 2000

Robbins, Anthony, *Unlimited Power*, New York, Fawcet, 1987

www.easystop.com

Printed in the United Kingdom by
Lightning Source UK Ltd., Milton Keynes
140902UK00001B/38/A